On Location

ON LOCATION
Settings from Famous Children's Books — #1

Joanne Kelly

Photographs by
Charles Kelly

Drawings and maps by
Pat Martin

1992
TEACHER IDEAS PRESS
A Division of
Libraries Unlimited, Inc.
Englewood, Colorado

For Chuck, Bud, and Doug,
my three men.

TEACHER IDEAS PRESS
A Division of
Libraries Unlimited, Inc.
P.O. Box 6633
Englewood, CO 80155-6633

Library of Congress Cataloging-in-Publication Data

Kelly, Joanne.
    On location : settings from famous children's books, #1 / Joanne Kelly ; photographs by Charles Kelly ; drawings and maps by Pat Martin.
    xv, 129 p. 22x28 cm.
    Includes bibliographical references and index.
    ISBN 1-56308-023-0
    1. Children's stories, American--Outlines, syllabi, etc.
2. Children--Books and reading. 3. Setting (Literature) I. Title.
PS374.C454K44 1992
813.009'9282--dc20   92-23553
                                                         CIP

Contents

Maps

Acknowledgments

Gathering the information for this book has been an enriching experience because of the generous assistance and interesting material shared by several talented and enthusiastic individuals. My sincere thanks to John Russell of Menomonie, Wisconsin; Walter Dietrick and Mark Scarborogh of Edgerton, Wisconsin; and Loren Poe of Newton, Illinois.

Introduction

In *Little House in the Big Woods*, author Laura Ingalls Wilder has a good definition of setting. She says "in those days and in that place" when describing some of the speech patterns used by the Ingalls family. And that definition can open the door to a look at children's literature that branches out from the stories themselves.

Many years ago, when my two sons were still boys, our family shared the hilarious misadventures of a raccoon named Rascal and the poignant story of a boy named Sterling (see *Rascal: A Memoir of a Better Era*, page 67). While vacationing in Wisconsin, we decided to try to locate the setting of the story, Sterling North's house in Edgerton, using the descriptions of places given in the book. Sterling North proved to be an accurate guide, and we were thrilled to find the house just where it should have been, near the church. In those days there was no sign to correctly identify our find, but there could be no mistaking it.

"Look! There's the bay window where Sterling put the Christmas tree!"
"Mom! There's Poe's steeple!"
"Gosh! I'll bet that's the very tree where Sterling built his hideaway."

That thrilling experience and the new perspective it gave us about the book and the area were not forgotten. As an elementary school librarian, I continued to investigate the possibilities of making the settings of good books come to life for my students. The school children and I visited locations within a reasonable distance and wrote to those farther away requesting information.

Children have always been excited about discovering how "the real place" actually looks, how it differs from the story setting, and how the author incorporated local features and history into the plot. Would it be possible to really go there, and what would you find if you did?

With some encouragement, children can use this information to increase their knowledge of the world around them by investigating the geography of the literary setting and contrasting it with what they already know of their own area. The possibilities for learning and for stimulating thinking skills are endless; however, care should be taken not to destroy a child's pleasure in the story itself. The activities suggested here should be shaped to fit the individual needs of students or adapted for the framework of the local curriculum.

The five books presented here span a broad range of reading levels. They are arranged progressively by level of difficulty, although there is certainly some overlapping, and they could arguably have been sequenced differently. Have fun with this book, and have a great time introducing children to the real places.

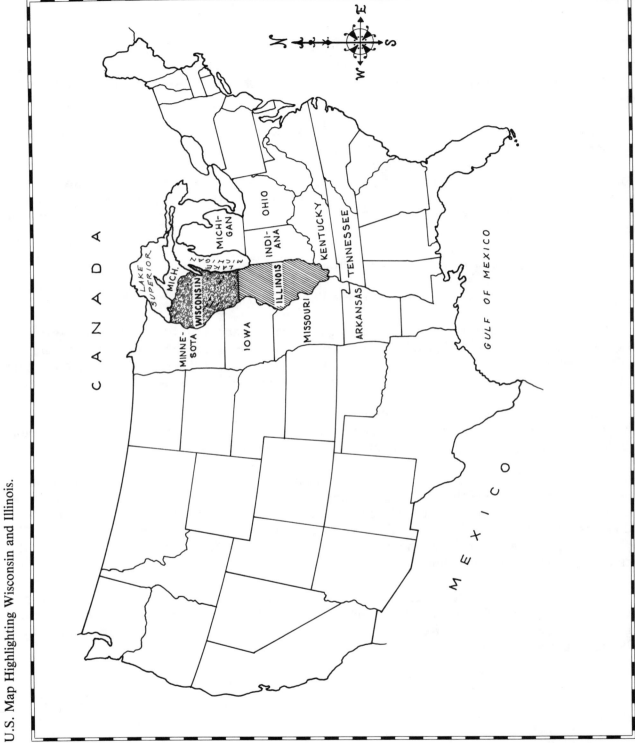

U.S. Map Highlighting Wisconsin and Illinois.

Wisconsin and Illinois.

Chapter 1 — Pepin, Wisconsin:
The Setting for Laura Ingalls Wilder's
Little House in the Big Woods

Illustrated by Garth Williams. Harper & Row, 1953. 238 pages.

BOOK SUMMARY

Laura Ingalls, born "in the Big Woods of Wisconsin in a little gray house made of logs" more than 100 years ago, has a baby sister, Carrie, and an older sister, Mary, who has beautiful golden curls and is always a very good little girl. Laura, on the other hand, has brown hair like her Pa's, and although she tries to be good most of the time, she has a spirited nature; Laura is every bit a normal little girl who just happens to be a young pioneer. In *Little House in the Big Woods*, an autobiographical story, the pioneer way of life is described through the eyes of this bright and questioning child.

The house in the Big Woods is far from neighbors but close to wild animals. Life is filled with chores for everyone in the family, but it is also filled with pleasures. During the course of a year, there are holidays and family gatherings, the wonders of springtime and harvest, trips to town, and cozy evenings of fun, songs, and storytelling in front of the fire. This is a classic, broadly appealing story of self-sufficiency in the wilderness amid the shelter and comfort of warm family ties.

ABOUT THE AUTHOR

Laura Ingalls Wilder is the author of a series of Little House books chronicling her childhood. She was born in the Little House in the Big Woods on February 7, 1867, and she traveled with her sisters and her pioneering parents to Kansas, Minnesota, and South Dakota. She attended log schoolhouses and pioneer churches; she experienced prairie fires, blizzards, and a plague of grasshoppers. She learned to value simple pleasures and to be cheerful and honest. She understood what it meant to have courage and to stand up for one's beliefs.

When Mary Ingalls lost her eyesight as a result of severe scarlet fever, Laura took on the responsibility of being her sister's "eyes." Wherever they went, Laura faithfully described everything she saw so that Mary could "see" it, too. More than ever, Laura looked carefully and reported honestly. Perhaps it was that training that sharpened her perception and developed her ability to communicate with simplicity and clarity.

DeSmet, South Dakota, where the Ingalls family later moved, was the Little Town on the Prairie where Laura grew to young womanhood, taught school, and met and married Almanzo (or Manly) Wilder. When Laura had been married for several years, she, her husband Almanzo, and their little girl, Rose, moved to a farm near Mansfield, Missouri, and there the pioneer girl who had lived in so many different homes settled down at last.

When her daughter had grown up and become a successful author, Laura thought Rose might enjoy some old family stories, so she jotted down a few and mailed them off to her. Several months later Rose wrote to her mother to say that her editor thought the stories could be made into children's books if Laura would "put some meat on the bones." Laura set about the task, and so began the famous series of Little House books about Laura, Mary, Ma, and Pa and their family and friends.

SETTING: PEPIN, WISCONSIN

Little House in the Big Woods is set in Pepin, Wisconsin, a small town at the widening of the Mississippi River called Lake Pepin about 65 miles northwest of La Crosse, Wisconsin, and 60 miles southeast of Minneapolis—St. Paul, Minnesota.

Pepin in 1862

When the Ingalls family arrived in Pepin in 1862, it was a boomtown. The pioneers of the day anticipated that it would become a flourishing city, "Queen City of Lake Pepin," the "Gate City of the Chippewa." It was an important and busy port for travelers and the lumbering industry. Investment opportunities were everywhere and land values were rising. There were three hotels, two banks, several stores, a newspaper, a cemetery, a post office, a Methodist church, a doctor's office, and a school where a Mrs. Louisa Ingalls taught. There were mills on the river for grinding grain, and elevators for storing it. In 1858 Pepin had been chosen as the county seat, but in 1867 (the year Laura was born) that honor was transferred to Durand on the Chippewa River. The population in 1882 was 340.

In a March 1, 1862, article in *The Pepin County Press*, publisher U. B. Shaver described Pepin as follows. This poetic description was written the year the Ingalls family arrived in town.

> Broad fields lay extended in sunlight where but a short time before wild beasts formed their coverts and hunted their prey. Acre after acre waved with bending wheat and rye, and gleamed with the yellow sheen of ripening corn. Cabins dotted the hillsides and mill wheels flashed in the running streams. Ponderous rafts of pine lumber floated down our great inland sea and found a market hundreds of miles distant. Our village of Pepin, at length, sent up its busy hum and the air was alive with the sounds and voices of intelligent and independent industry.
>
> Pepin commenced with fair prospects, moderate wealth and sanguine hopes. At first its largest products were children.
>
> The scenery of a country has much to do with the contentment, health and prosperity of its citizens. Let us take a stand-point on one of the stupendous bluffs which form a beautiful background to our village. What a splendid panorama opens to our view. At once rich, grand, comprehensive and imposing, ever varying, but never decreasing in grandeur and magnificence.

In those days, family groups set out pioneering together, and Laura's family was no exception. The extended family that moved from the Concord, Wisconsin area included Grandma and Grandpa (Lansford and Laura Ingalls), their six sons, four daughters, two daughters-in-law, and one son-in-law. Among that group were Charles and Carolyn Ingalls, the Ma and Pa of the Little House stories. For a while, the whole family lived together in one log cabin that they built, but it wasn't long before Pa began looking for a piece of land to homestead. It is the little cabin he built in the midst of the deep, dark woods that Laura describes in *Little House in the Big Woods*. She doesn't, however, mention the hills and valleys that are so distinctive and beautiful in this western part of Wisconsin, so different from the flat prairie where she would spend most of her girlhood after the family moved when she was six years old.

High land was the place to build a cabin, safe from the dangers of flooded creeks and with occasional spaces that opened to the sun. Pa chose a hilltop for their first home.

In 1863 Pa and Uncle Henry Quiner, Ma's brother, bought 80 acres of land on a wagon road 7 miles northwest of Pepin. They split the land in half, with the Ingalls family taking the south half and the Quiners the north. Pa and Uncle Henry soon set about building cabins.

Figure 1.1 shows the reconstruction of Laura's little house, built on 3 acres of the original homesite. The house Pa built stood for many years and even served as a corncrib before it disappeared.

FIG. 1.1. A reconstruction of Laura's Little House in the Big Woods.

Laura's comfortable house had a large attic that was a nice place to play. Downstairs there was a bedroom (left), a pantry, and a big room with two doors and two windows (see fig. 1.2).

FIG. 1.2. Cabin interior showing the bedroom (left) and the pantry (right).

In the big room (see fig. 1.3) was the large stone fireplace where Laura loved to watch the fire flickering and changing colors while Pa told stories on cold winter nights.

FIG. 1.3. The fireplace in the big room.

In the fall the pantry was crowded with barrels of salted fish and yellow cheeses stacked on the shelves in preparation for winter (see fig. 1.4).

FIG. 1.4. The pantry.

The Little House was surrounded by a crooked rail fence, to keep the wild animals away. One night, while Pa was away, Ma reached across that fence to slap what she thought was Sukey the cow. It wasn't the cow; it was a bear. Though the original fence is no longer standing, a new rail fence protects the site of the Little House today (see fig. 1.5).

FIG. 1.5. This rail fence protects the Little House Wayside.

Laura said that a wagon track ran through the deep woods in front of her house. Today that track is County Road CC, which winds through this still-beautiful woodland.

Maybe this wagon track in figure 1.6 that now runs near County Road CC looks the way the road past Laura's house did in 1867.

FIG. 1.6. A wooded wagon track near the Little House Wayside.

When Laura was four years old, she and Mary went to the log schoolhouse that was close to her home. It was District School No. 3, called the Barry School. It stood on this grassy knoll (see fig. 1.7) less than half a mile west of her home. The teacher was Miss Anna Barry. The Barry family had a farm at the crossroads, which became known as Barry Corner. Daughter Anna began her teaching career in the little log-cabin school in 1870 after receiving her teaching certificate in 1869. She had one year of experience when Laura, Mary, and cousin Charlie Quiner enrolled in October 1871.

About a mile down the road to the south and around the corner to the east is a newer Barry Corner School (fig. 1.8) built after the Ingalls family moved from the Big Woods. Laura and Mary never attended this brick schoolhouse, although some earlier studies assumed that they did.

FIG. 1.8. The "newer" Barry Corner School.

When Pa walked to Pepin or when the whole family rode there in the wagon, they traveled on what was then called the Lost Creek Road, now County Road CC. Lost Creek still tumbles cheerfully beside the road not far from the Little House (see fig. 1.9).

FIG. 1.9. Lost Creek.

Pepin, the first town that six-year-old Laura ever saw, was 7 miles from Laura's home. The town stood on the shores of Lake Pepin, which she described as vast and blue, stretching to the edge of the world. It is still considered one of the loveliest spots in Wisconsin.

Laura spent a wonderful afternoon on this beach in figure 1.10, gathering so many pretty pebbles that the pocket she stored them in tore out of her dress. The beach is now supervised by a lifeguard, but it is still peaceful and enjoyed by children.

FIG. 1.10. Lake Pepin and Laura's beach.

Just beyond that beach, the view changes as a small marina extends along the shoreline next to First Street (see fig. 1.11). It was on First Street that the Ingalls family shopped in stores conveniently located for the boats that brought in the supplies.

FIG. 1.11. The marina and First Street in Pepin.

Pepin Today

Pepin is still a very quiet little town that hasn't grown a great deal since Laura and her family lived nearby more than 120 years ago (see fig. 1.12). The population today is 890. For the visitor there are three campgrounds, a motel, a guesthouse, five cafes, an ice cream parlor, marina, and a swimming beach. There are also antique shops, an art gallery, and shops featuring local crafts, as well as four churches, two banks, a post office, and a public library. On weekend evenings in the summer a horse-drawn carriage takes passengers for a ride along the river on First Street (see fig. 1.13).

FIG. 1.12. Pepin is still a peaceful little town.

Laura tells of Pa's trip to Lake Pepin to catch fish in a net. He returned home with a wagonload of fish, some of which they salted down in barrels for the winter. Fishing is still an important activity around Lake Pepin; there are fishing contests in winter and summer. The lake is 30 miles long and 3 miles wide at its widest point. It is a favorite place for sailing and waterskiing. The lake area is shown in figure 1.14.

FIG. 1.13. Street map of Pepin, Wisconsin (1992).

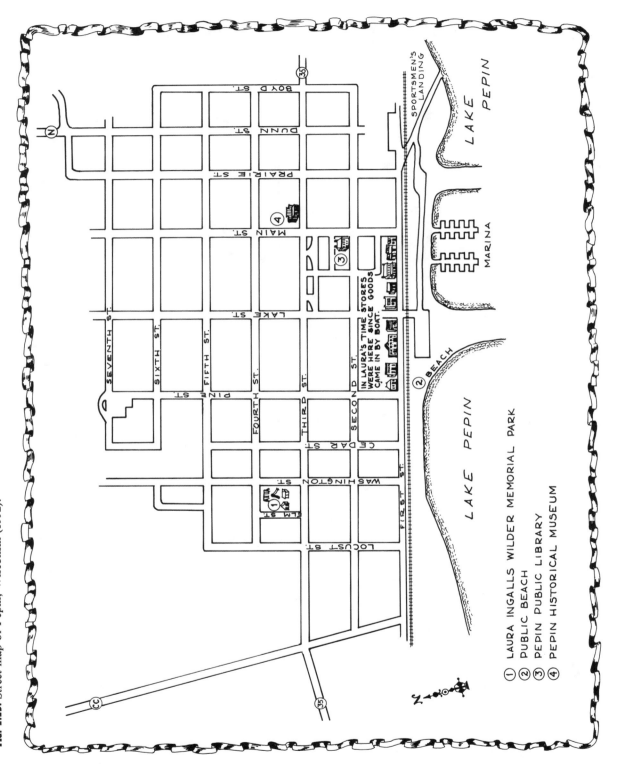

SEVENTH ST.

SIXTH ST.

FIFTH ST.

PINE ST.

FOURTH ST.

THIRD ST.

SECOND ST.

CEDAR ST.

WASHINGTON ST.

ELM ST.

LOCUST ST.

FIRST ST.

BOYD ST.

DUNN ST.

PRAIRIE ST.

MAIN ST.

LAKE ST.

IN LAURA'S TIME STORES WERE HERE SINCE GOODS CAME IN BY BOAT.

SPORTSMEN'S LANDING

LAKE PEPIN

MARINA

BEACH

LAKE PEPIN

N

CC

35

① LAURA INGALLS WILDER MEMORIAL PARK
② PUBLIC BEACH
③ PEPIN PUBLIC LIBRARY
④ PEPIN HISTORICAL MUSEUM

FIG. 1.14. The Lake Pepin area.

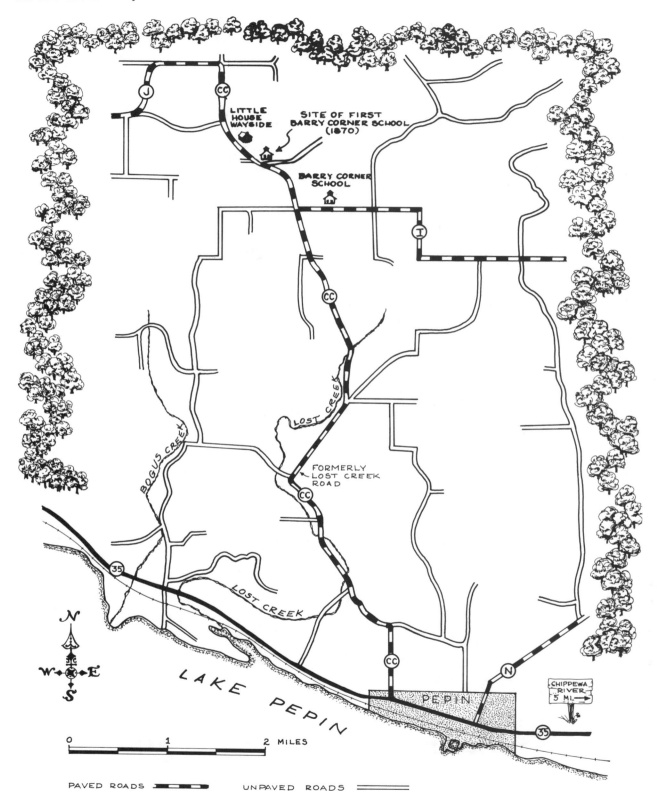

The citizens of Pepin are proud of their famous daughter, but it wasn't until 1961 when a St. Paul librarian wrote to the town urging them to commemorate Laura's birthplace that local interest in Laura Ingalls Wilder was truly sparked. That year the library committee began a search for the actual site of the Little House in the Big Woods. Old abstracts and maps of the area were studied until the names of Charles Ingalls and Henry Quiner were identified. In September 1863 they had purchased a quarter section of land from Charles Nunn. The 80 acres were near Lost Creek Road, 7 miles northwest of Pepin.

On September 16, 1962, a historical marker (see fig. 1.15) was unveiled in the town park in Pepin. The library board sponsored the marker, and the city renamed the park the Laura Ingalls Wilder Memorial Park. The dedication of the park and the unveiling of the marker were the high point of a two-day harvest festival.

FIG. 1.15. This marker identifies the Laura Ingalls Wilder Memorial Park.

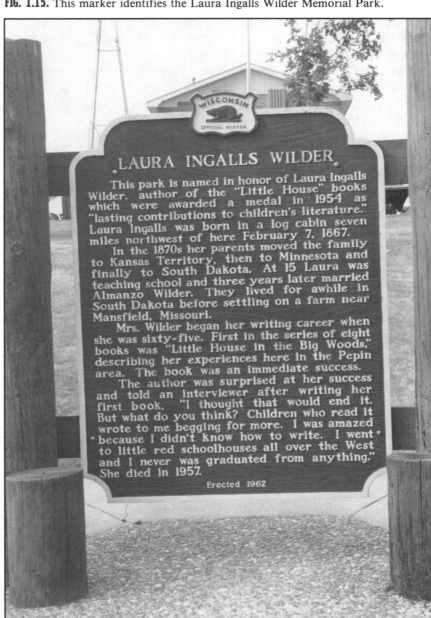

Organized in 1974, the Laura Ingalls Wilder Memorial Society was granted an official charter by the State Historical Society of Wisconsin in 1975. The society was given 3 acres of land at the site of the original Ingalls cabin, where members planned to build a replica of that cabin and to create a wayside park. A "Pennies for Laura" campaign was undertaken, and children from all over Wisconsin and neighboring states contributed so that a replica of Laura's first home could be constructed. In 1976 that work was completed.

The society tried to re-create the cabin that Laura describes in her book. Two oak trees were planted in the front yard, but cat holes weren't cut into the front door because small wild animals like raccoons and skunks might get in and use the cabin as a winter home. Most of the time the Little House is empty, but for special occasions the house is furnished the way it would have been in the 1860s and Society members dress in period costumes. Two such events were the dedication ceremonies in 1979 and the 10-year anniversary of the society in 1984.

The interior holds a display of documents relating to the Ingalls years in Pepin, including a copy of the Barry School register showing Laura, Mary, and cousin Charlie as pupils during the fall of 1871. There is a copy of the deed Pa and Uncle Henry signed for their land, photographs of the family, letters from Laura, and other information.

With the help of a federal grant, a well and visitor shelter, a historical marker, and a fence were added in 1978. In 1979 the society held an official dedication of the Little House Wayside and a celebration of their fifth anniversary as an organization. Plans currently are underway for a major restoration of the 16-year-old cabin during the summer of 1992.

The society also operates the Pepin Historical Museum on Highway 35 in town. The museum displays feature Pepin history and Laura Ingalls Wilder.

FOR MORE INFORMATION

Pepin Historical Museum
306 3rd St.
Pepin, WI 54759

Laura Ingalls Wilder Memorial Society, Inc.
Box 269
Pepin, WI 54759

EXTENDED ACTIVITIES

1. In what ways did the Big Woods of Wisconsin supply the needs of Laura's family? How are those same needs met today in your community?

2. Draw two sets of maps or pictures to show how the town of Pepin and the site of the little house have changed since Laura lived there.

3. Do the following on map A—Wilder of the Pepin area:
    a. Locate the *Little House in the Big Woods* using the scale of miles and these directions: take County Road CC 7 miles out of town. On the right side of the road, draw a little log cabin.
    b. Locate the Barry School using these directions: take Lost Creek Road southeast from the cabin to the first turnoff on the left. The school was on the left side of the road. Draw a one-room schoolhouse at that spot.
    c. Color Lake Pepin and the Mississippi River blue.
    d. Color Lost Creek blue.
    e. Trace the route Laura and her family took from their house to Pepin.

4. Laura's family moved many times during her childhood. On a map of the United States mark the different places you and your classmates have lived. Also mark some of the places you have visited.

5. When the first pioneers arrived in Pepin County, they settled in what became the towns of Pepin and Durand. Why do you think they chose those locations?

6. Locate Pepin on a Wisconsin road map. Describe its location in terms of direction and distance from at least three major cities in Wisconsin or nearby states.

7. Using a map of Wisconsin, explain why "Lake" Pepin is really not the correct name for the piece of water that the town of Pepin is near.

8. In your school or public library find an atlas that has specialized maps of the United States. Use information from some of those maps to describe the climate, resources, and natural vegetation of the area around Pepin.

9. What outdoor recreational activities would be popular in Pepin today? Which ones are different from those of Laura's time?

From *On Location*, 1992. Teacher Ideas Press, a Division of Libraries Unlimited, P.O. Box 6633, Englewood, CO 80155-6633

Map A—Wilder

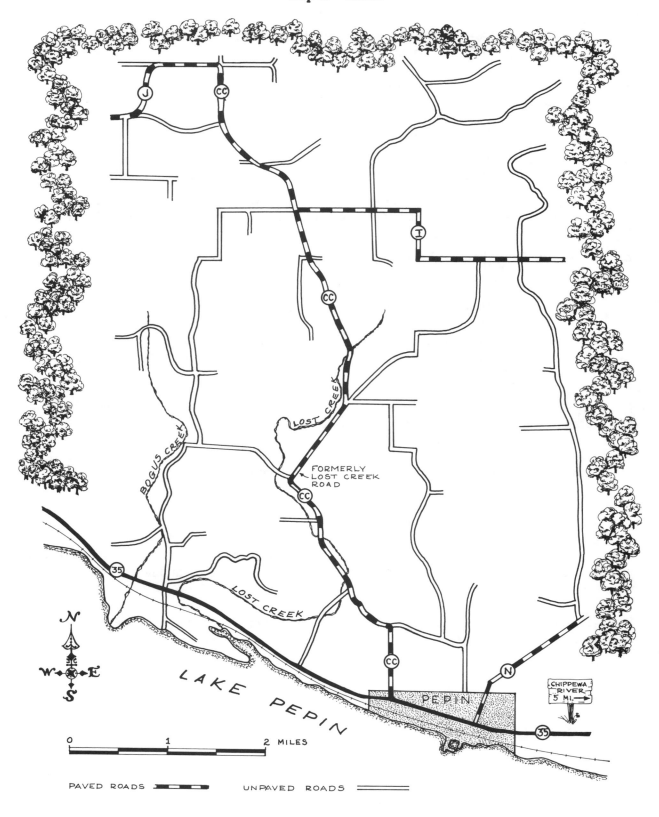

From *On Location*, 1992. Teacher Ideas Press, a Division of Libraries Unlimited, P.O. Box 6633, Englewood, CO 80155-6633

10. Compare the plants and wildlife of the *Little House* setting today with those of your region.

11. Pretend that you are a real estate agent who Pa has hired to sell the Little House in the Big Woods when the family moved to Minnesota. There is a family living in New York who might be interested in buying it, but first they want to know all about the house, the community, and the schools. Who lives in the area; what work do people do; and what means of travel do people use to get there? Write a letter to these big-city clients, answering their questions in a way that will persuade them to buy the property and move to the wilds of pioneer Wisconsin.

12. Use the scale on the floor plan of the Little House in the Big Woods (page 18) to calculate the size of the house and the dimensions of the rooms. Compare the room sizes with those of your classroom and the rooms of your home. Are there any rooms of similar size?

13. Laura tells us about some of the furniture in the Little House. Cut out and arrange these to-scale drawings of furniture (page 19) on the floor plan of the house as you think they would have been arranged in Laura's home. Consider the purpose of each piece and locate it where it would be most useful. What differences do you see between the furnishings in Laura's house and those in your home? How do you explain those differences? Would you like to live in the house? Why or why not?

Floor Plan for Little House in the Big Woods

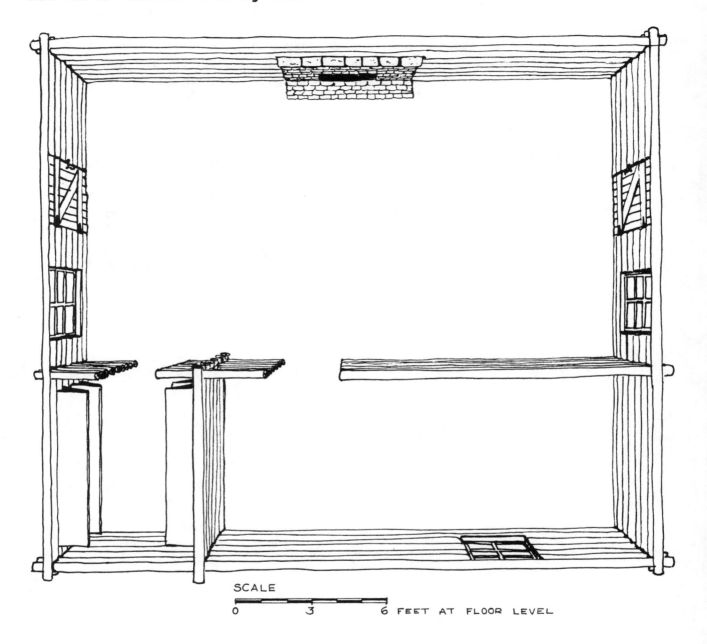

SCALE

0   3   6 FEET AT FLOOR LEVEL

From *On Location*, 1992. Teacher Ideas Press, a Division of Libraries Unlimited, P.O. Box 6633, Englewood, CO 80155-6633

Furniture for Little House in the Big Woods

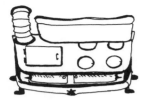

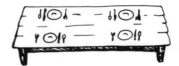

SUGGESTED READING

Other Books by Laura Ingalls Wilder

Little House on the Prairie. New York: Harper & Row, 1953. 334 pages.

The Ingalls family moves west in a covered wagon. They build a cabin in the Indian Territory of Kansas and Laura continues her homespun adventures.

On the Banks of Plum Creek. New York: Harper & Row, 1953. 338 pages.

When they move to Minnesota, Laura and her family live for a while in an underground dugout. Laura attends a town school, and the family survives a flood, a blizzard, and a plague of grasshoppers.

By the Shores of Silver Lake. New York: Harper & Row, 1953. 290 pages.

Construction of railway lines moves westward, and the Ingalls family follows because Pa has a new job at the railroad camp in South Dakota.

The Long Winter. New York: Harper & Row, 1953. 334 pages.

Laura is 14 when the family moves from their claim on the prairie into town. The winter is frighteningly severe, but Laura's new acquaintance, Almanzo (Manly) Wilder, helps the family survive.

Little Town on the Prairie. New York: Harper & Row, 1953. 304 pages.

Laura and Mary grow up in the prairie town of DeSmet, South Dakota, and Laura's days are filled with activities that include her family and friends.

These Happy Golden Years. New York: Harper & Row, 1953. 288 pages.

Laura begins teaching in a one-room country school at age 16. After her last term, she and Almanzo are married.

The First Four Years. New York: Harper, 1971. 134 pages.

This is the story of Laura's first years as a wife and mother as she and Almanzo homestead their claim on the South Dakota prairie.

On the Way Home. New York: Harper, 1962. 101 pages.

Laura kept a diary when her little family left South Dakota and traveled to Mansfield, Missouri. In that diary, which was discovered after her death, she carefully recorded the happiness, adventure, and sorrow that she encountered as she journeyed into a new land with Almanzo and seven-year-old Rose.

Letters from Home. New York: Harper, 1974. 124 pages.

In August 1915 Laura went on a trip to San Francisco to visit her daughter, Rose. Because Almanzo had to stay in Mansfield to take care of the farm, Laura sent him long letters telling him all about what she saw and, more importantly, what she thought of what she saw. These letters were found years after Laura's death.

Farmer Boy. New York: Harper & Row, 1953. 371 pages.

Here is the story of young Almanzo Wilder growing up in northern New York state.

Biographies of Laura Ingalls Wilder

Blair, Gwenda. *Laura Ingalls Wilder*. New York: Putnam, 1981. 64 pages.
   A brief and easy-to-read biography beginning with the move to the banks of Plum Creek in Minnesota.

Giff, Patricia Reilly. *Laura Ingalls Wilder: Growing Up in the Little House*. New York: Viking Penguin, 1987. 56 pages.
   Here is the story of how Laura wrote the books about her childhood and about her life with Manly on their Missouri farm.

Zochert, Donald. *Laura: The Life of Laura Ingalls Wilder*. Chicago: Contemporary Books, 1976. 260 pages.
   A thorough and factual treatment of the Ingalls family, rich in details and illustrated with family photographs.

Pioneer Cooking

Perl, Lila. *Hunter's Stew and Hangtown Fry, What Pioneer America Ate and Why*. Boston: Houghton Mifflin, 1977. 156 pages.
   Here is the story of the westward movement told through the cuisine of the nineteenth-century pioneers. Authentic recipes are included.

Schaeffer, Elizabeth. *Dandelion, Pokeweed, and Goosefoot: How the Early Settlers Used Plants for Food, Medicine, and in the Home*. New York: Young Scott, 1972. 94 pages.
   For their food and medicine, the settlers depended on many of the plants that we think of as weeds today. This book includes recipes as well as instructions for growing herbs.

Walker, Barbara Muhs. *The Little House Cookbook: Frontier Foods from Laura Ingalls Wilder's Classic Stories*. New York: Harper & Row, 1979. 240 pages.
   Learn how to re-create the food described in the Little House books. The recipes are here, along with quotes from the books and descriptions of food and cooking in pioneer days.

Pioneer Living

Alter, Judith. *Growing Up in the Old West*. New York: Franklin Watts, 1989. 64 pages.
   Generously illustrated with photographs, this interesting book describes the everyday life of settlers and the challenges and dangers of growing up in pioneer days.

Anderson, Joan. *Christmas on the Prairie*. New York: Clarion/Houghton Mifflin, 1985. unpaginated.
   Black-and-white photos and a simple text depict Christmas customs in a small, fictional Indiana frontier settlement in 1836.

Bealer, Alex W. *The Log Cabin: Homes of the North American Wilderness*. New York: Barre, 1987. 192 pages.
   In drawings and photographs, the floorplans and construction of log homes are described and log-cabin living is detailed.

Hilton, Suzanne. *Getting There: Pioneer Travel without Power*. Philadelphia, PA: Westminster Press, 1980. 192 pages.

An entertaining book about all modes of travel in frontier America, including horseback, stagecoach, canal boat, flat boat, covered wagon, and sailing ship.

Laycock, George. *How the Settlers Lived*. New York: McKay, 1980. 113 pages.

A detailed account of how settlers cleared forests, built homes, farmed, and hunted. Describes living conditions, clothing, and recreation.

Pioneer Music

Garson, Eugenia. *The Laura Ingalls Wilder Songbook*. New York: Harper & Row, 1968. 160 pages.

This book contains 62 of the songs and hymns sung by the Ingalls family as they crossed the plains. Background information is given for each song, along with the page of the story on which it appears.

Researching History

Cooper, Kay. *Who Put the Cannon in the Courthouse Square?* New York: Walker, 1984. 70 pages.

Learn how to follow clues and answer questions about the details of the past that are all around. Study examples of history projects and find out how to research and write parts of local history.

Weitzman, David L. *My Backyard History Book*. Boston: Little, Brown, 1975. 128 pages.

This book is filled with exciting activities and projects designed to show that history is all around, in the places we see and the things we do every day. Old photographs and silly sketches add to the fun.

Other Stories of Pioneers

Lane, Rose Wilder. *Let the Hurricane Roar*. New York: Harper, 1933, 1955. 118 pages.

A young pioneer family survives a plague of grasshoppers and winter blizzards. This story, originally published as *Young Pioneers*, is based upon some of Laura Ingalls Wilder's experiences as told by her daughter Rose.

Chapter 2 — Oglesby, Illinois:
The Setting for Marion Dane Bauer's
On My Honor

Clarion Books, 1986. 90 pages.

BOOK SUMMARY

It is a hot summer day when Tony talks Joel into a day-long bike trip to Starved Rock State Park. Joel doesn't really want to go at all. It is too far, and Tony's crazy plan to climb Starved Rock Bluffs is scary and dangerous. Even though he would rather go swimming in the city pool, Joel puts aside his misgivings and goes along. He doesn't want happy-go-lucky Tony to call him a chicken.

In a last-ditch attempt to thwart the planned trip and feeling very confident that his father will forbid the scheme, Joel asks permission to go. He is surprised when his father consents, asking only that Joel promise, on his honor, to go nowhere except the park and to be careful.

As the twelve-year-olds bike across the bridge spanning the dangerous Vermilion River, Tony suddenly changes his mind and suggests they go swimming. Joel is jubilant, until he realizes that Tony intends to swim in the Vermilion, not in the clean and safe city pool. The river water is filthy, the current too swift, and although he is a good swimmer, Joel is scared.

Maybe it is the challenge; maybe it is the fact that he has to prove something to himself and to Tony that makes Joel forget his caution and dare Tony to a race to the sandbar in the middle of the river. With a bit of a struggle, Joel makes the sandbar, but when he pulls himself out of the water and turns to taunt old slowpoke Tony, the river is empty, its surface still. Tony has vanished.

In the horrifying moments that follow, Joel repeatedly attempts to find his friend. Even the heroic underwater rescue efforts of a passing teenage driver bring no sign of Tony, and Joel is forced to admit to himself that Tony has drowned.

Wracked with grief, guilt, and anger at his father for approving the trip, Joel cannot face telling anyone what happened. Instead of reporting the accident to the police, Joel goes home and hides in his empty house, pretending to sleep. When his father comes home, Joel tells him that the park was too far and that he was tired and came home while Tony continued on.

Tony's parents become concerned when he doesn't come home, and Joel repeats the story to them. Late that night the police arrive, having discovered Tony's clothes and the bike at the river. Confronted with the anguish of Tony's parents, Joel finally relates the events of the tragic day and then attempts to withdraw into himself. When he learns his friend didn't really know how to swim, Joel feels even more responsible for the tragedy.

With love and understanding, Joel's father helps him confront the truth and begin to heal.

ABOUT THE AUTHOR

In 1938 Marion Dane Bauer was born in the small, Illinois prairie town of Oglesby, the daughter of a kindergarten teacher and a chemist. She attended local schools and the LaSalle-Peru-Oglesby Junior College. She continued her education at the University of Missouri and received a bachelor's degree from the University of Oklahoma in 1962. She has been a high school English teacher and an instructor in creative writing for adult education programs.

Ms. Bauer is the mother of two children and lives in a suburb of Minneapolis, Minnesota. The author of seven novels for young people, she has received many literary awards including the Golden Kite Award and the Jane Addams Children's Book Award. *On My Honor* was named a Newbery Honor book in 1987.

Marion Dane Bauer states that she always sets her novels in places she has lived or knows very well.[1] She also says that her books are based on her own life experience, although none are truly autobiographical.[2] *On My Honor* relates an actual event — a friend of Ms. Bauer's was with a boy who drowned in the Vermilion River — and takes place in Oglesby, Illinois, her childhood home.

SETTING: OGLESBY, ILLINOIS

Oglesby is a quiet Illinois prairie town with a population of about 4,000.

It is only 2 miles from the twin industrial towns of LaSalle and Peru (see fig. 2.1), and many of the residents of Oglesby work in those larger cities but prefer to live in Oglesby on quiet, tree-lined streets that run down to the riverside.

Oglesby's major industry is the large cement factory on the southern edge of the city on the banks of the Vermilion River. The town is almost completely encircled by the river (see fig. 2.2) and is less than a mile from the point at which the Vermilion empties into the larger Illinois River. It is hard to be very far from the riverbanks no matter where you are in Oglesby.

When Tony and Joel started out for Starved Rock State Park they were on their way to a beautiful, historic area (see the map in fig. 2.1). Joel remembered that the park's name comes from the legend of the band of Illinois American Indians who were driven to the top of a huge, rocky bluff by Potowatomi warriors. Trapped on the bluff, the Illinois band chose to starve rather than surrender.

FIG. 2.1. Area around Oglesby, Illinois.

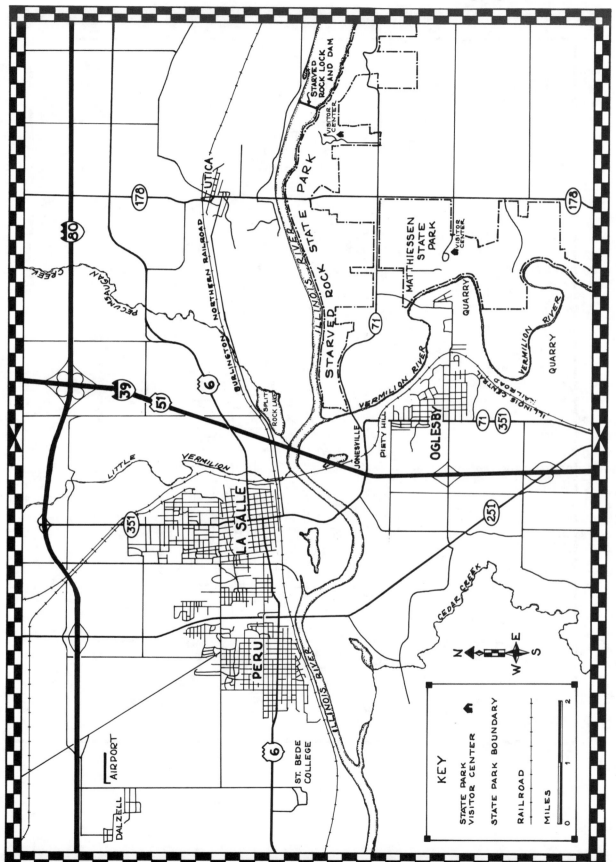

BASED ON MAPS PUBLISHED BY DELORME MAPPING, FREEPORT, MAINE, 1991

KEY

STATE PARK
VISITOR CENTER

STATE PARK BOUNDARY

RAILROAD

MILES

0   1   2

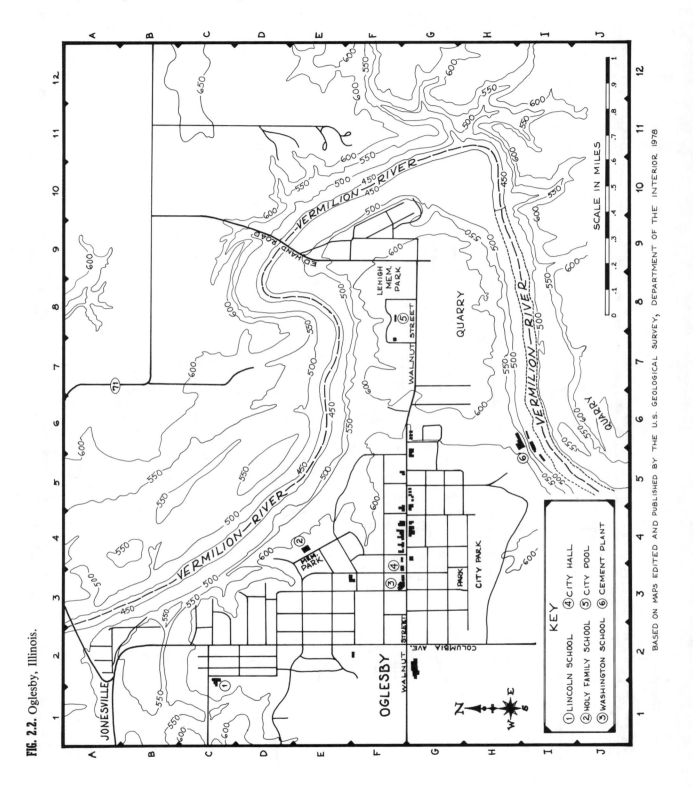

FIG. 2.2. Oglesby, Illinois.

The bluffs Tony was determined to climb are high, extremely dangerous, and strictly off-limits to climbers (see fig. 2.3). Joel was correct when he remembered that many people have been seriously injured in the park.

FIG. 2.3. Starved Rock.

Although Joel was pleased that Tony changed his mind about the reckless adventure to Starved Rock, he was not happy with the idea of swimming in the Vermilion River, either. The *Illinois Canoeing Guide*, published by the Illinois Department of Conservation, describes the Vermilion as a "wild river ... beyond doubt the best whitewater stream in Illinois." The portion of river at the Marquette Cement Factory, just south of the bridge where Joel and Tony swam, is known as a very dangerous spot for canoers. The guide advises that "this stretch is very dangerous and should be avoided by the novice."[3]

The road Tony and Joel followed out of town is the Ed Hand Road, which runs alongside Lehigh Park and then curves and sweeps down to the bridge over the Vermilion (see fig. 2.4). On the other side of the river, the road ascends a steep hill. Knowing this, Joel tried to gather enough momentum on the downhill side to negotiate this sharp climb. He was stalled, though, because Tony stopped on the bridge to peer down at the water.

FIG. 2.4. The Ed Hand Road sweeps down to the Vermilion River bridge.

Figure 2.5 shows the view Tony and Joel saw from the bridge.

FIG. 2.5. The view of the river from the bridge.

This area is particularly remote, with a wildlife refuge along the river and no houses in the vicinity (see fig. 2.6).

FIG. 2.6. The riverbank area is a wildlife refuge.

Joel and Tony left their bikes in the weeds along the side of the road and fought their way through the underbrush down the embankment to the river's edge beneath the bridge. Today a concrete spillway makes the going a little easier (see fig. 2.7).

FIG. 2.7. The river's edge beneath the bridge.

The glassy surface of the water (see fig. 2.8) hides the treacherous current below. It was in this direction that the boys swam—upstream, against that current. It isn't difficult to imagine a disaster happening under these circumstances.

FIG. 2.8. The deceptively placid surface of the Vermilion River.

FOR MORE INFORMATION

Illinois Valley Area Chamber of Commerce
P.O. Box 446
LaSalle, IL 61301

Starved Rock State Park
P.O. Box 116
Utica, IL 61373

NOTES

[1]Sally Holmes Holtze, ed., *Fifth Book of Junior Authors and Illustrators* (Bronx, N.Y.: H. W. Wilson, 1983), 25.

[2]Hal May and James G. Lesniak, eds., *Contemporary Authors*, New Revision Series, vol. 26 (Detroit: Gale Research, 1989), 40.

[3]*Illinois Canoeing Guide* (Springfield: Illinois Department of Conservation, 1980), 56 and 58.

EXTENDED ACTIVITIES

1. Joel cannot remember where the water from the Vermilion River goes after it empties into the Illinois. Use a map of the United States to trace the continuous flow of water from Oglesby to the ocean.

    a. Name all the rivers through which that water flows on its way to the sea.

    b. Name all the states that that water touches on its way to the sea.

2. There are actually three Vermilion Rivers in Illinois. List all the counties through which each of them flows.

    a. Vermilion River

    b. Little Vermilion

    c. Vermilion (South)

3. Refer to the two area maps (map A—Bauer and map B—Bauer) and locate all the forms of transportation shown.

4. Using a map of your hometown area, locate all the forms of transportation available nearby.

5. Again using the two maps of the Oglesby area, locate all the parks and recreation areas.

6. Locate all the parks and recreation areas on a local map of your area. Place a star by the parks you go to the most.

7. Joel claims that the bike ride to Starved Rock State Park is 10 or 12 miles, but his fathers says it is closer to 8 or 9. Use the scale of miles on the map of the Oglesby area to calculate the actual mileage from City Hall to the visitor's center at the park:

    a. First, use the route originally suggested: State Route 71 north to Jonesville, then 71 east to the park.

    b. Then, use the route the boys actually followed: Walnut Street east to Ed Hand Road, then north to Route 71.

    Who is closer to being correct, Joel or his father?

8. Using the map of Oglesby (map A—Bauer), give the map coordinates for:

    a. the swimming pool

    b. Washington School

    c. Lincoln School

    d. Holy Family School

From *On Location*, 1992. Teacher Ideas Press, a Division of Libraries Unlimited, P.O. Box 6633, Englewood, CO 80155-6633

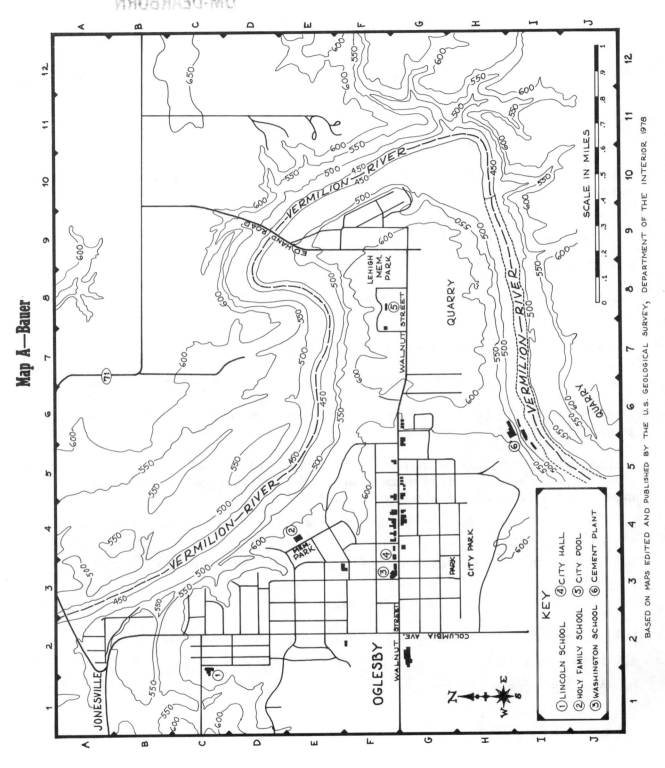

Map A—Bauer

KEY

① LINCOLN SCHOOL   ④ CITY HALL
② HOLY FAMILY SCHOOL   ⑤ CITY POOL
③ WASHINGTON SCHOOL   ⑥ CEMENT PLANT

SCALE IN MILES

BASED ON MAPS EDITED AND PUBLISHED BY THE U.S. GEOLOGICAL SURVEY, DEPARTMENT OF THE INTERIOR 1978

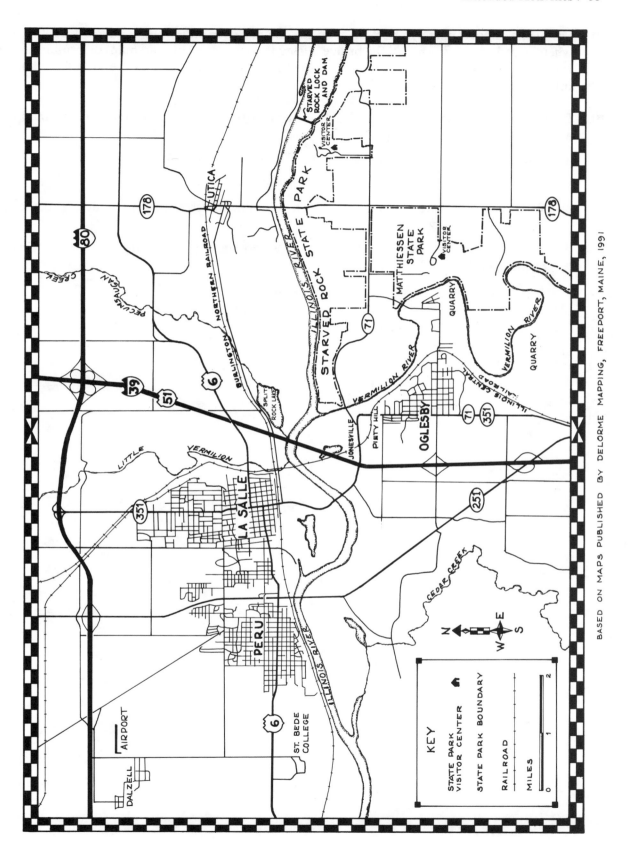

Map B—Bauer

9. Using the topographic symbols on map A—Bauer, determine how many feet Joel descended when he rode down the hill to the bridge. Using the same symbols and map, determine how many feet he would have climbed if he had pushed his bike up the road to the top of the hill on the other side of the bridge.

10. Examine map C—Bauer of the bedrock geology of the Illinois River area. Use the map keys to answer the following questions:

    a. The rocks of what geologic time period lie under the town of Oglesby?

    b. That period yields what major mineral resources?

    c. What connection can be made between the mineral resources of the area and the largest industry in the town?

    d. Are there links between the resources of an area and the industry of an area? Give some examples.

Map C—Bauer

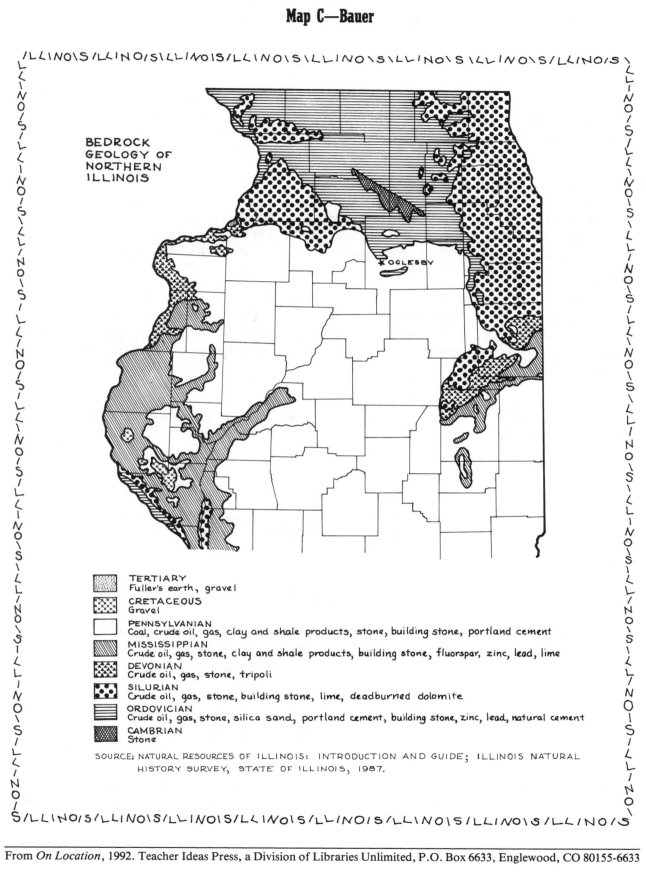

BEDROCK
GEOLOGY OF
NORTHERN
ILLINOIS

★ OGLESBY

TERTIARY
Fuller's earth, gravel

CRETACEOUS
Gravel

PENNSYLVANIAN
Coal, crude oil, gas, clay and shale products, stone, building stone, portland cement

MISSISSIPPIAN
Crude oil, gas, stone, clay and shale products, building stone, fluorspar, zinc, lead, lime

DEVONIAN
Crude oil, gas, stone, tripoli

SILURIAN
Crude oil, gas, stone, building stone, lime, deadburned dolomite

ORDOVICIAN
Crude oil, gas, stone, silica sand, portland cement, building stone, zinc, lead, natural cement

CAMBRIAN
Stone

SOURCE: NATURAL RESOURCES OF ILLINOIS: INTRODUCTION AND GUIDE; ILLINOIS NATURAL
HISTORY SURVEY, STATE OF ILLINOIS, 1987.

SUGGESTED READING

Other Books by Marion Dane Bauer

Foster Child. New York: Seabury, 1977. 153 pages.

A starkly realistic story of a young adolescent girl named Renny who has been abandoned by her parents and raised by a great-grandmother. Placed in a foster home after her great-grandmother is hospitalized with a stroke, Renny barely escapes sexual abuse by her foster father, a stern, religious fanatic, and she is forced to make some very adult decisions.

Like Mother, Like Daughter. Boston: Houghton Mifflin, 1985. 141 pages.

Leslie is ashamed of her soft-hearted, unconventional mother, but she admires her glamorous, outspoken teacher, Ms. Perl, who is also the advisor for the school newspaper. Encouraged by Ms. Perl to conduct a survey to see whether students feel they are learning anything in school, Leslie's unkind newspaper article causes the resignation of a math teacher and Ms. Perl's dismissal. Leslie learns to look beyond superficial appearances in people and to value the quality of caring for others.

Rain of Fire. New York: Clarion Books, 1983. 153 pages.

During the summer following the end of World War II, a boy discovers that all the talk of glory and heroism have little to do with the realities of war and the devastation that it brings. He finds that he must accept the consequences of his actions and that his own battles with his peers can also take a sobering toll.

Shelter from the Wind. New York: Seabury, 1976. 108 pages.

Stacy is angry with her father for remarrying, and she doesn't like her new stepmother or the fact that there will soon be a new baby in the family. She runs away from home and wanders on the Oklahoma plains until she is befriended by an old woman who helps her to better understand herself and the way things are.

Touch the Moon. New York: Clarion Books, 1987. 77 pages.

Jennifer, who longs for a real horse of her own, is bitterly disappointed when her father gives her a small, white, china figurine of one instead. The china horse turns into a real one named Moonseeker, who can even talk to Jennifer.

The Starved Rock Area

Ayars, James. *The Illinois River*. New York: Holt, Rinehart and Winston, 1968. 183 pages.

This book traces the history of the river and the Starved Rock area, including the legend of the Illinois American Indians who were trapped on the cliff. The modern area is described, and a special chapter gives information on things to do and see along the river.

Coping with the Death of a Friend

Blos, Joan. *A Gathering of Days*. New York: Scribner's, 1979. 144 pages.

This is the journal of 13-year-old Catherine Hall, a motherless girl who lives with her hardworking father and younger sister in New Hampshire in 1830. Cath's life changes dramatically when her father brings home a new wife, and Cassie, Cath's best friend, suddenly dies.

Boyd, Candy. *Breadsticks and Blessing Places*. New York: Macmillan, 1985. 210 pages.

Toni is a black sixth-grader in Chicago who is studying hard to pass the difficult entrance exam for a college preparatory school. Her problems suddenly seem small when her best friend is killed in an accident. It isn't until she comes to terms with her grief that she is able to function and live again.

Byars, Betsy. *Good-bye, Chicken Little*. New York: Harper & Row, 1979. 101 pages.

Jimmy tries in vain to stop Uncle Pete from taking the dare to cross the ice on the river. When Uncle Pete dies, Jimmy is sure that he is to blame.

Paterson, Katherine. *Bridge to Terabithia*. New York: Crowell, 1977. 128 pages.

Jess and Leslie are an unlikely pair of best friends, but Leslie has shown Jess a beautiful side of life. When Leslie dies accidentally, Jess learns to cope with overwhelming grief.

Smith, Doris. *A Taste of Blackberries*. New York: Crowell, 1973. 58 pages.

In exploring why his friend died, a boy discovers there is not always a logical answer.

White, E. B. *Charlotte's Web*. New York: Harper & Row, 1952. 184 pages.

Wilbur the pig faces the death of his friend Charlotte, a spider, with dignity and hope for the future.

Chapter 3 — Dunnville, Wisconsin:

The Setting for Carol Ryrie Brink's

Caddie Woodlawn

Macmillan, 1935, 1975. 270 pages.

Magical Melons: More Stories about Caddie Woodlawn

Macmillan, 1939. 193 pages.

BOOK SUMMARIES

Caddie Woodlawn

Growing up on the edge of the wilderness in the 1860s may have been a hardship for some, but not for an 11-year-old tomboy named Caddie Woodlawn. For Caddie, frontier life is one glorious escapade after another. One of six Woodlawn children, red-headed Caddie, who was sickly as a baby, has been allowed to grow up unrestricted by the usual rules of decorum for young women. She explores the Wisconsin countryside with her two brothers and leads them in unladylike but hilarious pranks. When younger brother Warren dares her to skate on thin ice, Caddie takes the dare but plunges into the freezing river. Quick action by her big brother Tom saves her life, and she emerges as spunky as ever. When a fussy, snobbish young relative from Boston visits to view the "quaint and rustic" pioneer way of life, Caddie and her brothers plot to give Annabelle an unforgettable frontier experience.

Caddie attends a one-room log schoolhouse, confronts the town bully, and comforts some lonely, rejected little waifs badly in need of love. She builds a lasting friendship with American Indian neighbors, making a perilous nighttime journey to warn them when hostile settlers seem about to attack. When irresponsible Uncle Edmund takes her dog to St. Louis to be trained for hunting and then loses him in the city, Caddie mourns the loss of her beloved pet. After several months Nero returns home, and the whole family, especially Caddie, rejoices.

In one memorable year Caddie learns to think for herself, to stand up for what she believes in, and to face the future cheerfully.

Magical Melons: More Stories about Caddie Woodlawn

Each of the six Woodlawn children is featured in at least one story in this collection, but Caddie is still the liveliest of the family. These stories span the years 1863 to 1866 and include the year of *Caddie Woodlawn*.

ABOUT THE AUTHOR

Carol Ryrie Brink was a five-year-old in Moscow, Idaho, when her father died in 1901. When her mother passed away three years later, Carol went to live with her grandmother and an unmarried aunt. That grandmother, Caddie Woodhouse, on whom the character Caddie Woodlawn was based, often entertained her lonely little granddaughter with the uproarious tales of her pioneer childhood in western Wisconsin. Carol loved those stories and tucked them away, in infinite detail, in her memory.

Carol attended schools in California, Oregon, and Washington before enrolling in the University of Idaho. She spent her senior year at the University of California, Berkeley, where she received her undergraduate degree.

Shortly after graduation she married Raymond Brink, a mathematics professor, and they moved to Minnesota, where he taught at the University of Minnesota at Minneapolis. They had two children, a son and daughter, and the family spent several years in Europe. Their experiences traveling in France formed the basis for her first book, *Anything Can Happen on the River*, published by Macmillan in 1934.

Carol Brink had always loved the stories her grandmother told about growing up in pioneer Wisconsin, so she made a trip to the town where Caddie Woodhouse and her family had lived in the 1860s. At the courthouse in Menomonie, she examined the tax records for 1864-1865 and discovered the location of the original family home in Dunnville. She later found many of the sites that were included in her grandmother's stories.

Mrs. Brink decided that perhaps other children would enjoy those tales as much as she had and she began work on a book. When composing the story based on the childhood adventures of her grandmother, Carol Ryrie Brink retained the authentic place names of the setting but changed personal names to some degree: thus the Woodhouse family became the Woodlawns of the book (their first names, however, were all accurately retained). While she was writing *Caddie Woodlawn*, Mrs. Brink frequently corresponded with the real Caddie, clarifying details, checking facts, and listening to suggestions. When *Caddie Woodlawn* was awarded the Newbery Medal in 1936, it was tremendously satisfying for both Carol Brink and her grandmother.

Carol Ryrie Brink continued to write, both for children and adults, producing short stories, plays, and poetry in addition to her many highly acclaimed juvenile novels. She died in La Jolla, California, on August 15, 1981.

SETTING: DUNNVILLE, WISCONSIN

Dunnville in 1857

Dunnville lies approximately 14 miles south of Menomonie, Wisconsin, and 20 miles east of Eau Claire, Wisconsin. Its location at the confluence of the Red Cedar (or Menomonie) and Chippewa rivers made it an ideal place for shipping and travel in Caddie's day. Steamboats chugging up the Mississippi and the Chippewa would make regular stops at Dunnville, and at the time, the town was the transportation hub of the region.

By 1854 the village had been designated the county seat of Dunn County. In those days the county boundary extended all the way to the Mississippi River and included present-day Pepin County, the site of Laura Ingalls Wilder's *Little House in the Big Woods* (see fig. 3.1). During the next few years the town prospered. Stores, hotels, and offices were built as the lumbering industry became established throughout the region.

FIG. 3.1. Dunn County, including present-day Pepin County.

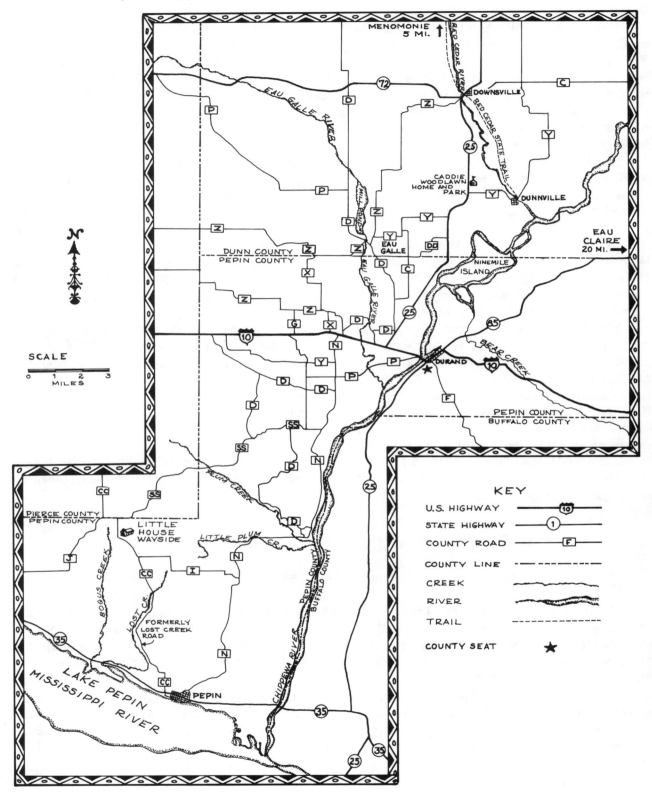

It was in 1857 that John Woodhouse and his wife, Harriet, brought their family of five children to the Wisconsin wilderness, a land of deep woodlands, Native American tribes, few trails, and fewer settlements. Behind them they left comfortable, cultured Boston, as well as beloved family and friends. Mr. Woodhouse had come to the frontier as a millwright to establish a sawmill for the Carson and Rand Company at a tiny settlement on the Eau Galle River.

Five Woodhouse children made the long, perilous journey to Wisconsin in 1857: Clara, Mary, Tom, Caddie, and Warren. Perhaps weakened by the difficulties of the trip, Mary died shortly after the family arrived. She was seven years old.

Caddie's health was delicate, and it may have been fear for her survival that prompted her parents to adopt a certain leniency in her upbringing, allowing Caddie to grow up free of the traditional constraints that bound proper young ladies of the time. Instead of sitting in the house stitching a sampler, Caddie ran and played in the fresh air and sunshine with her brothers, Tom and Warren. Clara, along with little sisters Hetty and Minnie who were born in Wisconsin, were proud of being little ladies and were often shocked at Caddie's wild ways.

The Woodhouse homestead was just outside the town of Dunnville. Miraculously, the house still stands (see fig. 3.2). It was discovered by Carol Ryrie Brink on a pilgrimage to the area while researching *Caddie Woodlawn*. She found the region (see fig. 3.3) had changed little since the 1860s; even today, the hills and valleys of "Caddie country" seem locked in a friendlier, less harried era.

FIG. 3.2. The Woodhouse home.

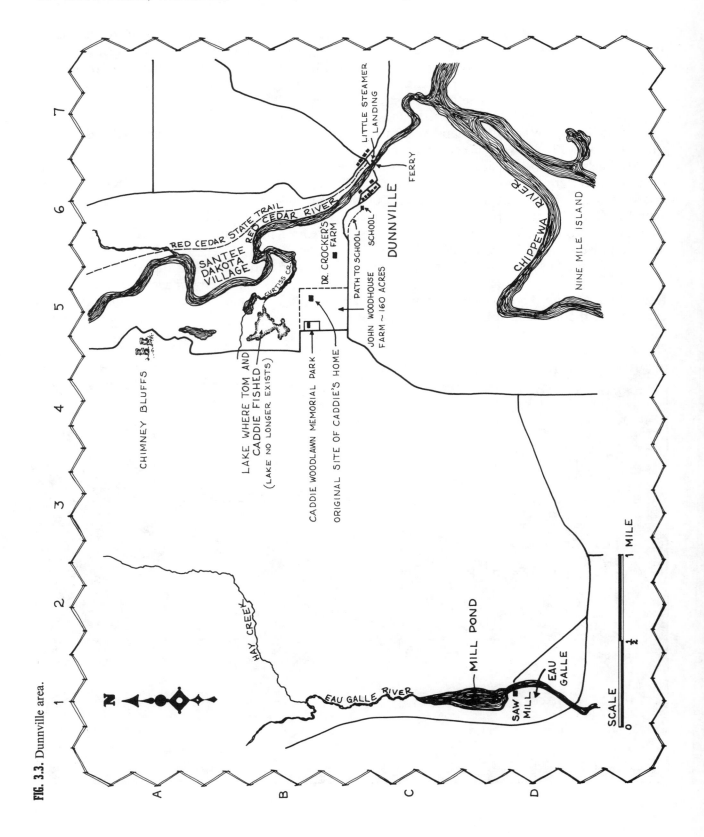

FIG. 3.3. Dunnville area.

The home originally stood about 300 yards to the east of the present location, near the tree line beyond this fence (see fig. 3.4). Both spots were part of the 160 acres owned and farmed by the Woodhouses.

FIG. 3.4. Original site of Caddie's house.

FIG. 3.4. Original site of Caddie's house.

The sawn-board house was originally built in 1856 by Levi Drake and purchased by John Woodhouse in 1860. It has changed a little in the 135 years since it was constructed, and Caddie's bedroom windows can still be seen on the second floor (see fig. 3.5).

FIG. 3.5. Caddie's bedroom windows are on the second floor.

One major change has been the removal of the large kitchen wing that used to extend from the west side of the house. Above it was the attic where Caddie and her father repaired clocks. Where there is now an upstairs bedroom window, there used to be a door that led to that attic; the small, present-day porch is where the door that led to the kitchen used to be (see fig. 3.6). The kitchen wing was pulled off to serve as a henhouse for later owners. Figure 3.7 shows a floor plan of the house as Caddie may have known it.

FIG. 3.6. A kitchen wing used to extend from this side of the house.

FIG. 3.7. Floorplan of the Woodhouse home.

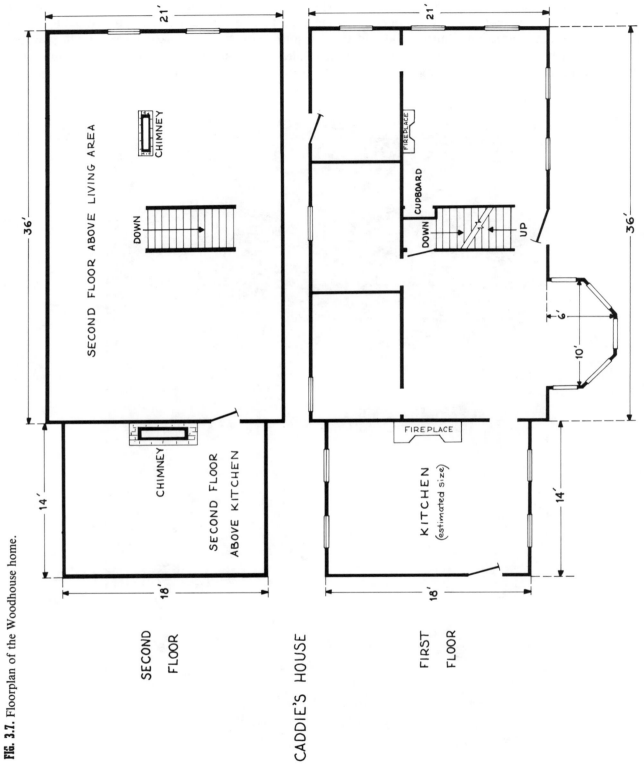

SECOND FLOOR ABOVE LIVING AREA

CHIMNEY

DOWN

CHIMNEY

SECOND FLOOR ABOVE KITCHEN

36'

21'

14'

18'

SECOND FLOOR

FIREPLACE

CUPBOARD

DOWN

UP

DOWN

KITCHEN
(estimated size)

FIREPLACE

6'

10'

36'

21'

14'

18'

CADDIE'S HOUSE

FIRST FLOOR

In the introduction to the 1973 edition of *Caddie Woodlawn*, Carol Ryrie Brink says that all the names in the tale except one are changed to some extent. The only unchanged name belonged to Robert Ireton, the hired man. Brink thought that because farm laborers often moved from place to place, no one would remember him. He is remembered, however, and his grave can still be found in the Riverview cemetery just east of Downsville, to the north of Dunnville (see fig. 3.8).

FIG. 3.8. Robert Ireton's grave.

Nearly all the events that are described in *Caddie Woodlawn* and *Magical Melons* are based on actual occurrences. The "Indian Massacre Scare" reported in *Caddie Woodlawn* actually took place in August 1862, and just as in the story, it was a false alarm. The Native Americans were minding their own business on their own land, not plotting an uprising. Nevertheless, when a vat of soap boiled over, the smoke was seen by some children, who spread the rumor that the American Indians were on the attack. The citizens of Dunnville were warned of impending trouble, and this incident inspired the episode in the book when the settlers gathered at the Woodlawn farm for mutual protection. Caddie overheard some hot-headed neighbors hatching a plan to gather the frightened settlers and attack the Native American camp. Fearing for her friends in the Santee Dakota tribe, Caddie made a daring nighttime ride over the countryside and across the frozen river to warn Indian John of the impending danger. The American Indian camp was about 2 miles from the Woodhouse home, in a woodland clearing on the other side of the Red Cedar River. Indian John, who actually existed, later moved to Maiden Rock, Wisconsin, on the Mississippi River near Pepin, and lived to be more than 100 years old. He died in 1912, a respected member of the community.

It was to this clearing (see fig. 3.9) that Caddie raced to warn Indian John of the impending settler attack. Present-day owners report finding many arrowheads and other relics in the area.

FIG. 3.9. Site of the Santee Dakota camp.

The path that Caddie, Tom, Warren, and Hetty walked to school (see fig. 3.10) can still be seen winding up from the road on the south side of the Woodhouse property, through the wooded hillside to the schoolyard.

FIG. 3.10. Path the Woodhouse children took to school.

The frame schoolhouse the children attended (see fig. 3.11) was built in 1858 at a cost of $88.00. John Woodhouse served as the treasurer of School District No. 3 from 1862 until 1867. That building was moved in 1908, and on the same spot stands the brick schoolhouse built to replace it.

FIG. 3.11. The frame schoolhouse the Woodhouses attended.

The original wooden building, which Obediah Jones had saved from a fire in *Caddie Woodlawn*, did actually burn down in the 1930s.

One quiet summer day turned into an exciting adventure when Caddie, Tom, and Warren went blueberry picking at Chimney Bluffs. Tom was wildly happy when he discovered the skeleton of a rattlesnake, but when Caddie discovered a live rattler, all thoughts of blueberries vanished as the three raced down the bluff to the river. Neither blueberries nor rattlesnakes can be found around those sandstone outcroppings today, but Chimney Bluffs is still a challenging climb up steep slopes (see fig. 3.12).

FIG. 3.12. Chimney Bluffs.

The land just east of the Woodhouse property was owned by a Doctor Crocker, the first physician in the area. In *Magical Melons* he is portrayed as Dr. Nightingale, whose wife became Hetty's close friend. It was in the Nightingale parlor that Hetty discovered the curio cabinet that housed an amazing exhibit, and it was there also that she met Adelaide, the magnificently attired doll. Dr. Crocker is buried in a nearby pioneer cemetery; his office still stands in Dunnville.

John Woodhouse worked at the mill in the tiny settlement of Eau Galle. In *Magical Melons* Caddie, along with her friends and family, all rode in the hay wagon to the picnic grounds by the riverside in Eau Galle for the Fourth of July celebration. Caddie wistfully watched the boys in the greased pig contest, but she had vowed to act like a young lady and keep her new white dress, with its red-white-and-blue sash, neat and clean. But as everyone cheered for Robert Ireton in the log-rolling contest, Caddie spied little Ezra McCantry trying to balance on a slippery log at the river's edge. When the log began to roll, it took Ezra by surprise, and he splashed into the deep water. Caddie forgot her vow as she plunged into the current and struggled to save Ezra. The Eau Galle River still runs swift and deep through the picnic grounds at the edge of town (see fig. 3.13).

FIG. 3.13. The Eau Galle River as it runs past the picnic grounds.

The county courthouse, on the west side of Dunnville, burned down in 1858. Two years later the county seat was moved to Menomonie. Other towns in the area had large enough white pine forests to support local mills and encourage economic growth, but Dunnville did not. For a few years the village continued to serve as the steamboat landing for passengers and freight heading north, but when the railroad came through Dunnville to Menomonie in the 1880s, that river service was discontinued. Now, hardly a building remains in the town, and the dock site of the little steamer that brought goods, passengers, and news to the town has vanished. Stretching along the bank of the river was the town center, which included the Dunnville general store, built in 1854 by the lumber firm of Knapp, Stout and Company. It was in the general store that Caddie first met Indian John and here that she took the Hankinson children to buy a dollar's worth of candy, toys, combs, and handkerchiefs. The store and the hotel are gone now; only foundations lie hidden in the brush. A few houses and the school still stand on the other side of the river.

In 1867 the Woodhouse family left Dunnville and moved to St. Louis, Missouri. Caddie later met and married a young doctor. When they moved to the frontier territory of Idaho, Caddie once again became a pioneer.

Dunnville Today

In 1968, Dunn County citizens decided to establish a *Caddie Woodlawn* commemorative park, raising money through book and button sales, square dances, and a *Caddie Woodlawn* play. As a result of these efforts, travelers today can stop at this pleasant county park and actually enter the home where Caddie Woodhouse's family worked and played. The park is located on State Route 25, 12 miles south of Menomonie. The 5-acre park is part of the 160 acres originally owned and farmed by John Woodhouse. Notice that the name of the Newbery award has been misspelled on the commemorative plaque (see fig. 3.14).

FIG. 3.14. Plaque welcoming visitors to the Caddie Woodlawn park.

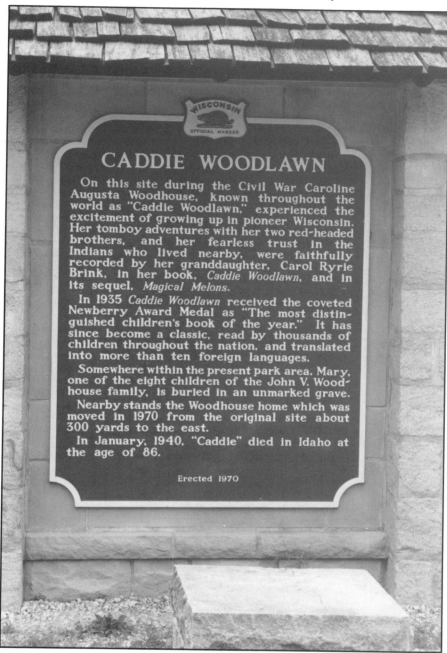

When the house was moved to its present park location in 1970, several interesting discoveries were made. This pair of old-fashioned shoes (see fig. 3.15) was found in a wall where they had fallen and been hidden for years. Even more intriguing was the discovery of a child-sized bow-and-arrow set tucked carefully away in the recesses of a wall.

FIG. 3.15. These old-fashioned shoes were discovered in a wall of Caddie's house.

The interior of the Woodhouse home is sunny and bright, for there are large windows in every room (see fig. 3.16). It's easy to imagine the family gathered around the table for dinner in the cozy dining room or Caddie clattering up the stairs to her second-floor room under the eaves.

FIG. 3.16. Large windows made Caddie's home sunny and bright.

When Caddie's older sister Mary died shortly after the family arrived from Boston, she was buried in an unmarked grave somewhere on the property. A memorial to Mary and other pioneer children has been erected near the house (see fig. 3.17).

FIG. 3.17. Memorial erected near the Woodhouse home.

Today, the town of Dunnville has nearly vanished. Only one street of houses remains, and all traces of the once-flourishing river traffic have vanished. Along the nearby riverbank is the beautiful Red Cedar State Trail that runs 14 miles from Menomonie to the Dunnville Wildlife Area.

In Downsville, 2 miles north of the park, is the Empire in Pine Museum, where maps of "Caddie Woodlawn country" can be found.

There is an interesting historical link between *Caddie Woodlawn* and Laura Ingalls Wilder. The "Little Steamer" that brought visitors and freight to the river port of Dunnville during Caddie's day was the *Pete Wilson*. Later, the boat, which was still operating in 1900, was renamed for its well-known captain, Phil Sheckle. When the lumbering trade left the Dunnville area, the steamer was sent to transport goods off the Florida coast. Today, the anchor of the *Phil Sheckle* is mounted in the park honoring Laura Ingalls Wilder in Pepin, Wisconsin (see fig. 3.18).

FIG. 3.18. Anchor of the *Phil Sheckle*.

FOR MORE INFORMATION

Caddie Woodlawn County Park
Highway 25
Downsville, WI 54735

Dunn County Historical Society
P.O. Box 437
Menomonie, WI 54751

Empire in Pine Museum
Downsville, WI 54735

Red Cedar State Trail
Rt. 6
P.O. Box 1
Menomonie, WI 54751

EXTENDED ACTIVITIES

1. Caddie Woodlawn and Laura Ingalls Wilder lived in the same part of Wisconsin. Mark the locations of both of their homes on map A—Brink of the area, then do the following:

   a. Mark the shortest route between the two homesteads.

   b. Use the scale of miles to calculate the distance between the two homes. One method used to measure routes that have many turns and twists is to lay a piece of string along the roads to be taken. Mark the beginning and ending points of the journey on the string. Next, extend the marked string along the scale of miles and measure the number of miles between the marks.

   c. Name the county where Caddie lived.

   d. Name the county where Laura lived, then name the county seat.

2. Locate Caddie's farm on map B—Brink, which shows the Dunnville area. Do the following:

   a. Find the number and letter coordinates for:

      1. Chimney Bluffs

      2. Santee Dakota village

      3. Eau Galle

      4. Dunnville School

   b. Mark the route Caddie probably took to warn Indian John that the settlers were about to attack. Remember, she cut across fields and woods, avoiding the road, and she crossed the frozen river over the ice, not relying on a bridge or ferry.

   c. Mark Father's probable route to work at the mill in Eau Galle. How far did he travel to work?

3. Is it possible that Caddie and Laura were friends? Why or why not?

4. Describe the changes that have taken place in Dunnville since Caddie lived there. How do you account for those changes?

5. Where did Uncle Edmund take Nero? On the regional map presented in map C—Brink:

   a. Show the river route they traveled to that destination and Nero's possible path back home

   b. Use the scale of miles to calculate the approximate mileage Nero traveled on his way back home.

6. In *Caddie Woodlawn*, Cousin Annabelle came from Boston to visit. Using map C—Brink, which shows the transportation routes available to travelers in the 1860s, plan a trip from Boston to Dunnville.

7. In your school or public library, find modern transportation maps of the United States that show railway and airline routes and major highways. How would you make the trip from Boston to Dunnville today?

From *On Location*, 1992. Teacher Ideas Press, a Division of Libraries Unlimited, P.O. Box 6633, Englewood, CO 80155-6633

Map A—Brink

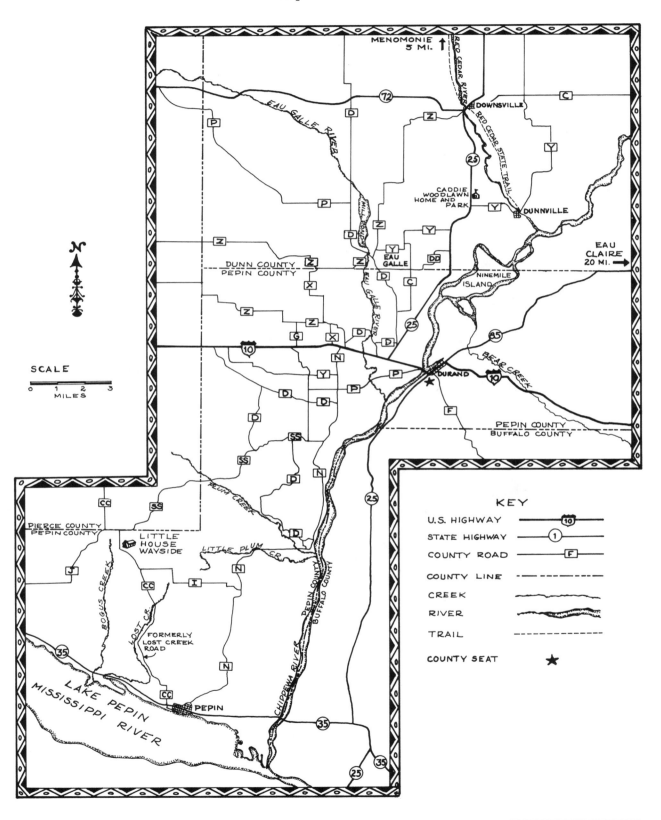

Map B—Brink

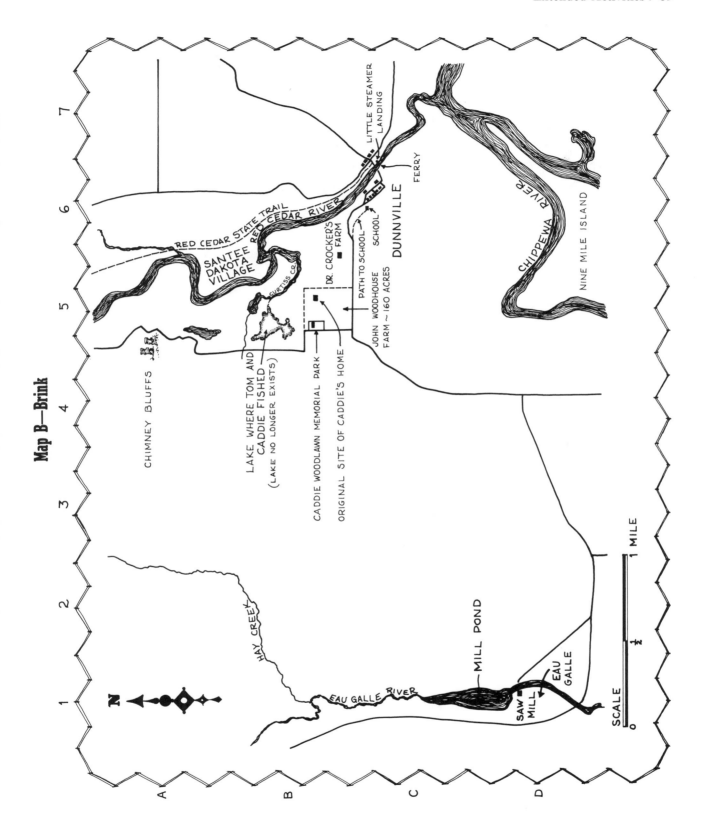

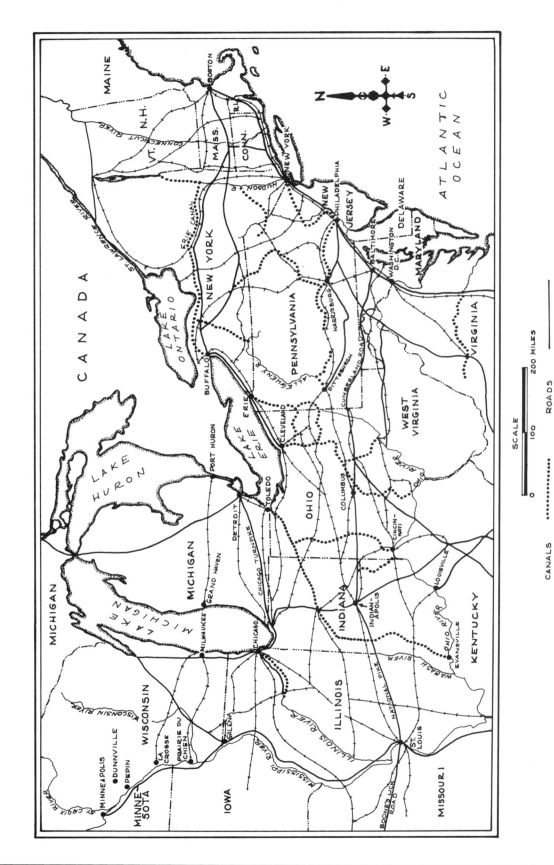

Map C—Brink

SELECTED TRANSPORTATION ROUTES DURING THE 1860s

8. Compare how long the trip might have taken in the 1860s and how long it would take today.

9. How did the Woodlawns learn of news from distant places? How does your family find out national and world news today?

10. Give an address for Caddie Woodlawn County Park that includes planet, hemisphere, continent, country, region, state, county, town, and road.

11. Describe the physical characteristics of the region that Caddie and Laura call home: the topographical features, climate, natural vegetation, and natural resources. Compare them to the physical characteristics of the region that you call home.

12. Compare the homes of Caddie Woodlawn and Laura Ingalls in the following ways:

    a. Determine the number of acres of farmland that each family owned.

    b. Determine the materials from which each home was constructed.

    c. Using the floor plans of Laura's house (page 62) and those of Caddie's house (page 63), determine the following:

        1. the overall size of each home

        2. the number of rooms in each home

        3. the number of windows in each home

        4. the number of fireplaces in each home

13. It is interesting to note that although the Woodhouse family actually lived in western Wisconsin before the Ingalls family had even arrived in Pepin and although Dunnville was in a more remote location, further from the centers of "civilization," the Ingalls family lived a more pioneering way of life than the Woodhouse family. How could this be? Consider the following factors in your answer:

    a. the distance of each home from the nearest town.

    b. the primary occupation of Laura's father and Caddie's father.

    c. the number of people in each household.

    d. the place each family had lived before coming to western Wisconsin (the Ingalls family had been pioneers in eastern Wisconsin, whereas the Woodhouse family had lived in Boston). What influence, if any, might that have had on the lifestyles of each family?

Floor Plan of the Ingalls Home

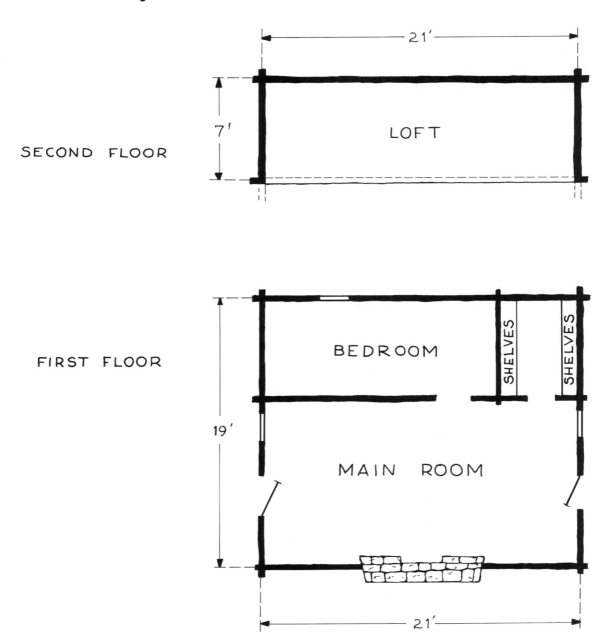

Floor Plan of the Woodhouse Home

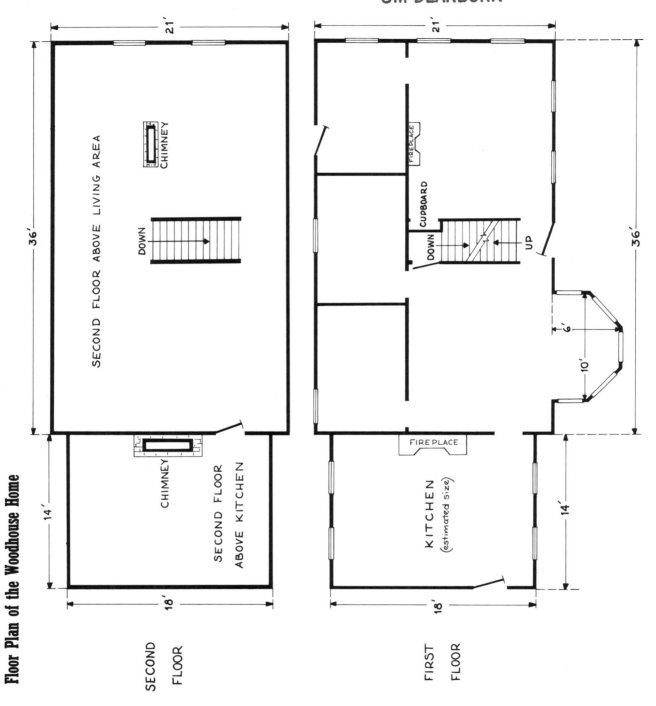

SECOND
FLOOR

FIRST
FLOOR

SUGGESTED READING

Other Books by Carol Ryrie Brink

All Over Town. New York: Macmillan, 1939. 291 pages.
  The setting is a turn-of-the-century small town where a doctor's daughter, along with her friends, finds lots of opportunity for adventure.

Andy Buckram's Tin Men. New York: Viking, 1966. 192 pages.
  Twelve-year-old Andy invents four robots and they really work! Then, during a flood, Andy and two other children are marooned on an island along with the robots.

Baby Island. New York: Macmillan, 1937. 172 pages.
  Laura and Mary are aboard an ocean liner headed for Australia, where they are supposed to meet their father. When the ship seems to be sinking, the girls, along with four babies, are hastily set adrift on a lifeboat. Laura and Mary bravely tackle the challenge of survival and the responsibility of caring for the babies and set up home on a tropical island.

The Bad Times of Irma Baumlein. New York: Macmillan, 1972. 134 pages.
  Irma, the new girl at school, tries to impress her classmates by claiming to own the world's largest doll. Trouble comes when she is asked to exhibit it.

Family Grandstand. New York: Macmillan, 1952. 208 pages.
  A university professor's family has a home with a tower that overlooks the football stadium, and they and their friends and neighbors all enjoy the view.

Family Sabbatical. New York: Viking, 1956. 256 pages.
  The professor and his family have traveled to France, where the children enjoy learning about other cultures and making new friends.

Winter Cottage. New York: Macmillan, 1968. 178 pages.
  The Depression has been hard on Minty, her father, and her little sister. Tired of moving from one rented room to another, the little family moves into a vacant summer cottage in Wisconsin in hopes of making a fresh start.

Clocks and Watches

Gibbons, Gail. *Clocks and How They Go*. New York: Crowell, 1979. unpaginated.
  The illustrations take the reader inside the mechanisms of the weight clock and the spring clock.

Johnson, Chester. *What Makes a Clock Tick?* New York: Little, Brown, 1969. 73 pages.
  Simple clocks are explained piece by piece, and readers can try rebuilding a clock.

Zubrowski, Bernie. *Clocks: Building and Experimenting with Model Timepieces*. New York: Morrow, 1988. 112 pages.
  A guide to clock building with step-by-step instructions and good illustrations.

Pioneer Children (Fiction)

Archer, Marion Fuller. *Keys for Signe*. Niles, IL: Albert Whitman, 1965. 160 pages.
   A shy, Norwegian immigrant girl finds life in 1868 Oshkosh, Wisconsin, to be exciting and challenging.

_____. *Sarah Jane*. Niles, IL: Albert Whitman, 1972. 190 pages.
   In 1852, 14-year-old Sarah Jane arrives from England expecting to meet her widowed father in Sheboygan, Wisconsin. Instead, he introduces her to his new wife, who can only speak Welsh.

Blos, Joan. *A Gathering of Days*. New York: Scribner's, 1979. 144 pages.
   This is the journal of 13-year-old Catherine Hall, a motherless girl who lives with her hardworking father and younger sister in New Hampshire in 1830. Cath's life changes dramatically when father brings home a new wife and Cassie, Cath's best friend, suddenly dies.

Speare, Elizabeth. *Sign of the Beaver*. Boston: Houghton Mifflin, 1983. 135 pages.
   When their wilderness cabin in Maine is completed, Matt's father returns home to get the rest of the family, but Matt remains to guard the new homestead. After a robber takes his provisions and gun, Matt is befriended by an American Indian and his son, who not only teach him how to survive but also bring him an understanding and respect for the Native American way of life.

Pioneer Life

Anderson, Joan. *Glorious Fourth at Prairietown*. New York: Morrow, 1986. unpaginated.
   This photoessay celebrates the Fourth of July in a fictional pioneer town.

Tunis, Edwin. *Frontier Living*. New York: Crowell, 1976. 168 pages.
   Detailed information is given about everyday life on the frontier and about the changes that occurred during the westward movement. Drawings illustrate descriptions of farming, hunting, housework, education, and more.

Wright, Louis. *Everyday Life on the American Frontier*. New York: Putnam, 1968. 256 pages.
   Details of the westward movement, illustrated with more than 130 engravings, lithographs, woodcuts, and prints from the period.

Researching History

Brownstone, Douglass L. *A Field Guide to America's History*. New York: Facts on File, 1984. 325 pages.
   Information on becoming an amateur historian in the community.

Chaney, Steven. *Kid's America*. New York: Workman, 1978. 414 pages.
   Here is a generous collection of activities and projects that introduce aspects of American life from the colonial period to the present.

Steamboats and Other Riverboats

Andrist, Ralph K. *Steamboats on the Mississippi*. New York: American Heritage, 1962. 153 pages.
Interesting episodes in the history of Mississippi steamboats. Includes sketches and well-illustrated descriptions of river transportation.

Ault, Phil. *Whistles Round the Bend: Travel on America's Waterways*. New York: Dodd, Mead, 1982. 192 pages.
A colorful history filled with exciting tales and interesting old prints, photographs, and maps.

McCall, Edith. *Mississippi Steamboatman: The Story of Henry Miller Shreve*. New York: Walker, 1985. 115 pages.
Shreve built a boat that could travel up the Mississippi River when Fulton's couldn't. Contains copies of maps and illustrations from the 1800s.

Chapter 4 — Edgerton, Wisconsin:
The Setting for Sterling North's
Rascal: A Memoir of a Better Era

Illustrated by John Schoenherr. Dutton, 1963. 180 pages.

BOOK SUMMARY

During one exciting, adventure-filled year of his youth, Sterling North had a pet raccoon. In his autobiographical account, he tells how this engaging, inquisitive coon helped dispel his loneliness. His mother had died, his two sisters were grown, his brother was fighting in World War I, and his permissive, absentminded father was often away. Understandably, 11-year-old Sterling eagerly accepted the companionship of the tiny, wild baby raccoon when it was discovered in a nest by Wowser, the family's St. Bernard. The responsibility of caring for a wild animal and keeping it as a pet had its hazards as well as its joys, and Sterling became experienced in both that summer of 1918.

ABOUT THE AUTHOR

It's not really surprising that Sterling North became a literary critic, an editor, and an author. He was the youngest child in a family that valued the written word. His mother, who at the age of 18 had graduated from college at the head of her class, was a linguist and a biologist. She taught her four children to read and write when they were very young. Sterling's older brother and sisters were prize-winning childhood poets. Sterling began his literary career at the age of eight when his poem "A Song of Summer" was published in *The St. Nicholas Magazine* in 1914. As a teenager he contributed poetry to *Harper's, The Nation*, and other literary magazines.

Sterling North's Wisconsin childhood was not without sadness. He was only seven when his mother died, and he was often lonely after his older sisters grew up and moved away. He described his father as an easygoing gentleman who had a wide range of talents and interests, a real-estate speculator who was also an expert on American Indian artifacts. In *Rascal*, Sterling's father is portrayed as well-meaning but rather absentminded and so permissive that neighbors were sometimes worried about Sterling's welfare.

Sterling's older brother fought in France during World War I (a cause of great concern to his family), and his father frequently traveled on business, so the youngster was often alone in the large home in Edgerton. His many pets became a surrogate family, and those sometimes happy, sometimes lonely days are described in *Rascal: A Memoir of a Better Era*, first published by Dutton in 1963.

Sterling continued writing as a teenager, but he had ambitions of becoming a prize-fighter and football player. Those dreams were cut short, however, when he contracted a severe case of infantile paralysis at the age of 15. Although he was warned that he might never walk again, Sterling recovered with only a slight limp.

At Edgerton High School, Sterling was strongly influenced by his talented English teacher, Margaret Stafford, and graduated in 1925 as class valedictorian. He worked his way through the University of Chicago by writing poetry and short stories for national magazines, doing bookkeeping for a sanitarium, working at an auto body factory, and raising and selling vegetables. In addition, he edited the campus literary magazine, helped operate an off-campus theater, received numerous literary awards, and had a book of poetry published by the University of Chicago Press. At the age of 20, he married his high school sweetheart, Gladys Buchanan.

In 1929 he joined the staff of the *Chicago Daily News* as a cub reporter and soon became its literary editor, a post he held for 12 years. In 1943 he moved to New York to become the literary editor of the *New York Post* and later held the same position with the *New York World Telegram and Sun*. From 1957 to 1964 he was the general editor of the North Star Books division of Houghton Mifflin.

After his first book was published in 1929, North wrote a book almost every year for the next 40 years, gaining recognition and receiving more awards. His novel *So Dear to My Heart* was a bestseller in 1947 and was filmed by Walt Disney in 1949. *Rascal* has been published in 14 other countries, has sold more than 2.5 million copies, and was filmed by Walt Disney Productions in 1969.

For many years North and his wife lived on their 27-acre miniature wildlife sanctuary near Morristown, New Jersey. There they enjoyed a small lake, a waterfall, virgin forest, and numerous foxes, deer, and, of course, raccoons.

Sterling North died in 1974 at the age of 68.

SETTING: EDGERTON, WISCONSIN

Sterling North's fictional town of Brailsford Junction is, in reality, his hometown of Edgerton, Wisconsin. It was in the woods at the edge of town that he found Rascal, his pet raccoon and close companion, and it was on the banks of a nearby creek that he said goodbye to his friend more than a year later.

Edgerton is located in south-central Wisconsin, about 30 miles southeast of Madison, the state capital, and 10 miles north of Janesville. Just a few miles away is Lake Koshkonong, one of Wisconsin's largest lakes, and it was in a farmhouse on the shores of this lake that Sterling North was born in 1906. In 1909 the family moved into Edgerton, which is shown in figure 4.1. The area of Wisconsin around Edgerton is shown in figure 4.2.

Edgerton in 1918

The Edgerton of 1918 was a bustling agricultural center referred to as "the Tobacco Capital of the World." The census of 1910 shows a population of 2,513, and by 1920 the town had grown to 2,688. There were 52 tobacco warehouses in Edgerton that dried and processed the crop, and business in that commodity was brisk. With the railroad running right through town and the Rock River wandering through fertile fields less than 2 miles away, the prosperity of the town seemed assured.

Sterling North's boyhood home still stands on West Rollin Street and despite the weathering of almost 75 years, it is still much as he describes it in the book.

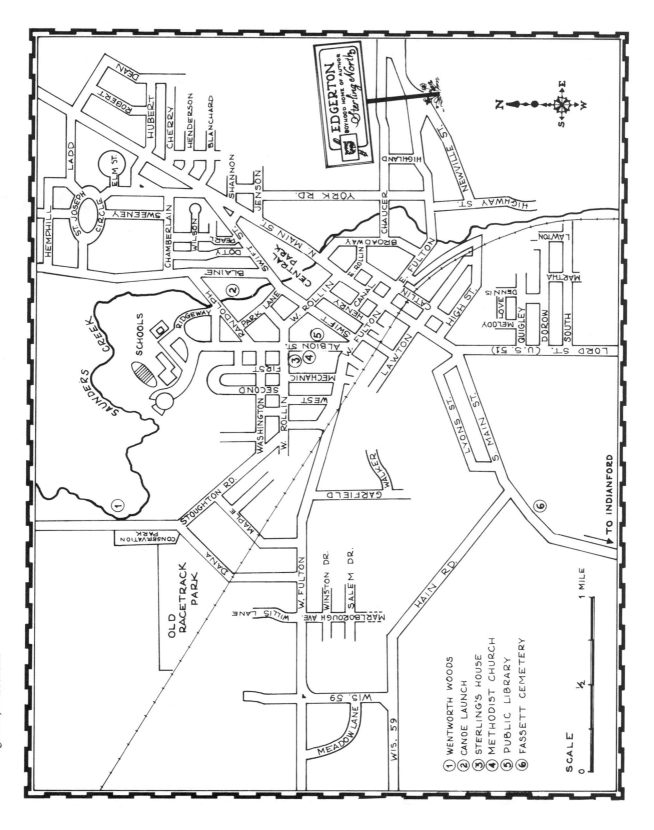

FIG. 4.1. Edgerton, Wisconsin.

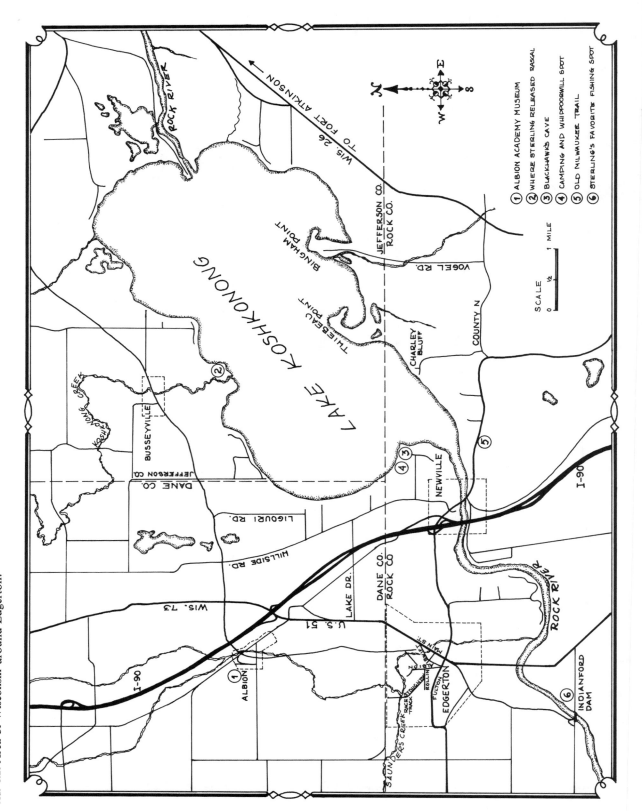

FIG. 4.2. Area of Wisconsin around Edgerton.

Sterling's upstairs bedroom window is there, as is the bay window where he secured the Christmas tree behind chicken wire so that Rascal would be unable to fondle those irresistible, shiny ornaments (see fig. 4.3).

FIG. 4.3. "There was a large semicircular bay extending from the livingroom ... where we always mounted our Christmas tree." (East side of house showing the bay window.) "Often the only occupant of our ten-room house was an eleven-year-old boy working on his canoe in the living room." From RASCAL by Sterling North. Copyright©1963 by Sterling North. Used by permission of Dutton Children's Books, a division of Penguin Books USA Inc.

In the backyard, the barn where Rascal lived still stands. When Sterling reluctantly built a cage for his "ringtailed wonder," he cut a small door in the west side of the barn to provide access to the box stall inside (see fig. 4.4).

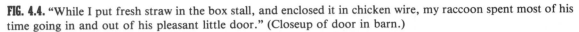

FIG. 4.4. "While I put fresh straw in the box stall, and enclosed it in chicken wire, my raccoon spent most of his time going in and out of his pleasant little door." (Closeup of door in barn.)

That opening still exists, as does the huge old oak tree where the baby raccoon spent the first few weeks of his new life in town (fig. 4.5).

FIG. 4.5. The oak tree, where Sterling and Rascal ate jelly sandwiches, was Rascal's favorite part of the backyard.

It is easy to imagine a boy and a raccoon relaxing and eating jelly sandwiches in the oak's enormous spreading branches that were perfect for climbing.

The kindly Reverend Hooton lived next door in the Methodist parsonage. It was he who suffered through the indiscretions of Sterling's pet skunks and patiently endured that raucous black thief, Poe-the-Crow. The house is still the parsonage for the Methodist church to the east (see fig. 4.6).

FIG. 4.6. "After any thievery he would travel by devious routes before slipping between the wide slats of the Methodist belfry where he presumably stored his loot." (The Methodist church bell tower was frequented by Poe-the-Crow.)

Poe-the-Crow's home was in the belfry of that church, and it was that 75-foot dark and dusty belfry (see fig. 4.7) that Sterling climbed in order to search in Poe's nest for his sister's engagement ring. The church and belfry remain, and that belfry, now proudly labeled as the home of Poe, is no less gloomy and forbidding than the day it was scaled by an 11-year-old boy.

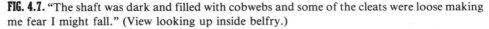

FIG. 4.7. "The shaft was dark and filled with cobwebs and some of the cleats were loose making me fear I might fall." (View looking up inside belfry.)

Rascal was found in Wentworth's woods, which hug the northwest side of Edgerton.

An overgrown trail leads into the woods (see fig. 4.8), where a small clearing provides a perfect location for spotting raccoons, imaginary or real. Just as the book describes, Saunders Creek runs nearby.

FIG. 4.8. " 'I'm headed for Wentworth's woods,' I told Oscar, 'and I may not start home before moonrise.' " (View of Wentworth's Woods Trail.)

Indianford (spelled Indian Ford in the book), was Sterling's favorite place to fish, and it is still reached by following Main Street south about 2 miles out of town. It was here that Sterling fished for bass, sunfish, and channel catfish at his favorite spot near a sandbar while Rascal caught crayfish. The river continues to pour over the dam in this quiet, beautiful place, still a favorite spot for anglers. There are sandbars and small islands aplenty here (see fig. 4.9), so visitors can only guess which one

FIG. 4.9. "We came at last to my secret fishing place, the sandbar with the deep and quiet hole below it where I had caught more fish than anywhere else in the river." (Photo of Indianford.)

might have been Sterling's, with its deep, dark pool off the point. Many years later his father moved to a home on the river at Indianford, and Sterling once hoped to build a summer home there, too.

Sterling's mother, whom he so lovingly describes in *Rascal*, is buried in a simple grave in Fassett Cemetery just south of town (see fig. 4.10). Sterling would have passed that cemetery every time he went to fish at Indianford. His easygoing, permissive father is buried next to her.

FIG. 4.10. "It seemed an inadequate tribute, only partially compensated by the roses I had planted there." (Mrs. North's gravestone.)

Two miles east of Edgerton is Lake Koshkonong (see fig. 4.11). It is 4 miles wide, 9 miles long, and covers 10,464 acres. The lakeshores were wooded in 1918, with miles of sand beaches. Sterling's father remembered that in the days of his childhood, American Indian wigwams stood on Crab Apple Point, Thiebeau's Point, and Charlie's Bluff. It was said that the chief of the Sac tribe, Black Hawk, fled from pursuers on the lake in 1832, and Sterling felt that he knew just where the chief had hidden.

FIG. 4.11. "This was our very own lake, filling our lives to the brim." (Lake Koshkonong.)

In August 1918 Sterling and his father took a car trip through Wisconsin to the shores of Lake Superior. Of course, Rascal went along. In those days there were few improved roads through rural Wisconsin, and the travelers intentionally explored the byways on a slow—and for Sterling, enlightening—journey (see fig. 4.12). They followed the Rock River to its source, then headed north to the Brule River, not far from Superior, Wisconsin.

FIG. 4.12. "In fact there was scant paving of any kind, only friendly little roads that wandered everywhere, muddy in wet weather, dusty in dry." (Dirt road near Brule River.)

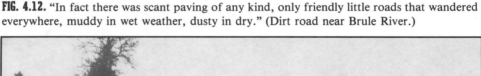

For two weeks they camped along the banks of the Brule, and many of those days Sterling and Rascal explored the river alone. Sterling's father was often occupied with court cases in Superior and had no misgivings about leaving Sterling to fend for himself for the day. During those days, Sterling fished and explored the woods and river to his heart's content.

The Brule River has long been known as a passageway between Lake Superior and the Mississippi River by way of the St. Croix and a tortuous portage connecting the Brule and St. Croix. Native Americans used the difficult route long before white men entered the territory, poling their canoes upstream against the current and portaging around the rapids. In 1907 the Brule River State Forest was established to protect the wilderness, and it remains a popular hiking and camping region today. The Brule is still considered an excellent trout stream (see fig. 4.13).

FIG. 4.13. "I was seeing enough big trout where the sun struck deep into the pools to know that here was a stream to rival Isaak Walton's River Dove." (View of the Brule River.)

After protecting, caring for, and cherishing his pet for almost a year, Sterling decided that it was time for Rascal to return to the wild. The boy had served as a wonderful foster parent. Rascal was 13 times the weight he had been when Sterling found him, and he was accomplished in the ways of raccoon survival.

The mouth of Koshkonong Creek was selected as a release point because of its remote location and the abundance of wildlife.

Sterling describes nearly a full day's journey by canoe, and a careful comparison of his route with the area map (fig. 4.2) will verify the distance and justify that time frame.

The site of Rascal's release at Koshkonong Point is still remote and wild. With no roads nearby, there is no access to the area except by boat. It seems especially fitting that the whole length of the creek, from Busseyville to the mouth at Lake Koshkonong, is now a Wisconsin State Game Farm. Sterling would be delighted to know that no hunting or trapping is allowed in the refuge.

Edgerton Today

Visiting Edgerton is easier today than it was when Sterling North lived there; Interstate 90 passes only 2 miles to the east. With its population of almost 4,400 expanding rapidly into the surrounding area, it is still a bustling agricultural center where the tobacco industry is important. Only a few of the original 52 tobacco warehouses remain, but the Tobacco City Museum displays items related to the tobacco trade.

Most of the homes and public and commercial buildings that Sterling knew still stand and have been carefully preserved.

Currently under restoration is the historic Carlton Hotel, built during the Victorian era, when tobacco barons negotiated business deals within its halls.

Sterling North's home at 409 West Rollin Street, owned by the Sterling North Society, is identified by an impressive marker that has an interesting history. In October 1982 a group of fifth-graders from Janesville, Wisconsin, read *Rascal* and were surprised to find that the story was set in Edgerton, just 10 miles away. When they discovered that the North home was not identified, they wrote to the Edgerton City Council, suggesting that a sign be erected so that readers would know where the story took place. They accompanied their suggestions with a petition bearing 44 signatures. The city council thought the idea was excellent and undertook a campaign to raise money for the marker.

Fourth- and fifth-graders at the Edgerton Elementary School enthusiastically joined the project and organized a roller-skating fund-raiser at the community center in March 1983. Sterling North's high school class made a donation in his memory, and groups of school children in Janesville, Wisconsin, and in New Jersey and Ohio sent contributions. The Edgerton Chamber of Commerce took over fund-raising efforts, and in 1984 a 20-by-40-inch brown-and-ivory metal marker was erected (see fig. 4.14). The dedication ceremony was attended by Sterling North's son and other dignitaries and

FIG. 4.14. Brown-and-ivory marker identifying Sterling North's home.

by a large group of schoolchildren from Edgerton and Janesville. To commemorate the event, a blueberry-pie-eating contest was held on the green of the Albion Academy. Children from 5 to 13 years old raced to be the first to finish eating blueberry pies without using their hands, just as Sterling and Rascal had done 66 years earlier.

In 1989 the Sterling North Society Ltd. was organized. Local sites related to North have been identified, and a map of Rascal sites has been published. Displays about Sterling North and his books are featured at the Edgerton Public Library. The Albion Academy Historical Museum, located just 4 miles north of Edgerton, houses one of the largest collections of North memorabilia in Wisconsin, including the paddle from his homemade canoe. That 18-foot-long canoe and other family artifacts were destroyed in a fire that raged through the academy in 1965.

FOR MORE INFORMATION

Sterling North Society Ltd.
P.O. Box 295
Edgerton, WI 53534

Edgerton Area Chamber of Commerce
P.O. Box 5
Edgerton, WI 53534

Edgerton Public Library
101 Albion Street
Edgerton, WI 53534

EXTENDED ACTIVITIES

1. Using the map of Edgerton (map A—North) and clues in this chapter and in *Rascal*, determine which numbers represent the following:

   a. Sterling's home

   b. the Methodist church

   c. Wentworth's Woods

   d. the cemetery where Sterling's mother is buried

   e. the waterway where the canoe was launched

   f. the public library where North displays are featured

2. Using map B—North of the Edgerton area and clues in this chapter and in *Rascal*, determine which numbers represent the following:

   a. Sterling's favorite fishing spot

   b. the place where Sterling released Rascal

   c. Black Hawk's cave

   d. the spot where Sterling and his father camped and looked for whippoorwills

   e. the old Milwaukee Trail

   f. the Albion Academy Museum

3. Use maps A— and B—North to determine

   a. how far Sterling walked to go to Wentworth's Woods

   b. how far Sterling rode his bike to Indian Ford

   c. how far Sterling paddled his canoe to release Rascal at Koshkonong Creek (hint: use a string to measure the length of the river, then measure the piece of string used)

   d. in which county Rascal was born

   e. in which county Rascal was released

   f. in which direction Sterling traveled when he went from his home to Indian Ford

   g. in which direction he traveled to release Rascal.

4. Using the description in the book, mark the 1927 Wisconsin highway map C—North (on page 84) to show the probable route Sterling and his father followed to the Brule River. (Caution: there are two Brule Rivers in Wisconsin. Using clues in the book, determine which Brule River the Norths visited.)

Map A—North

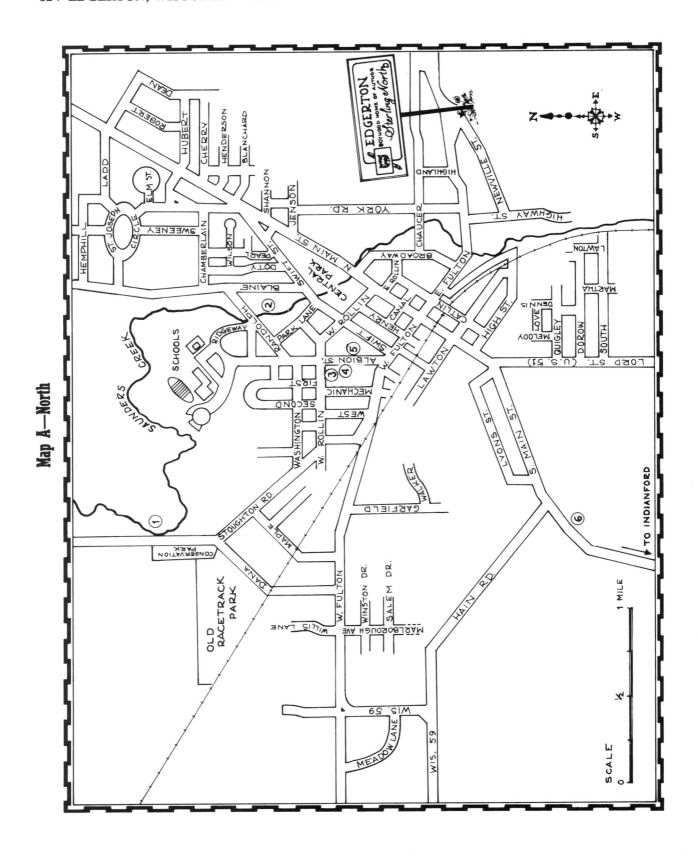

Map B—North

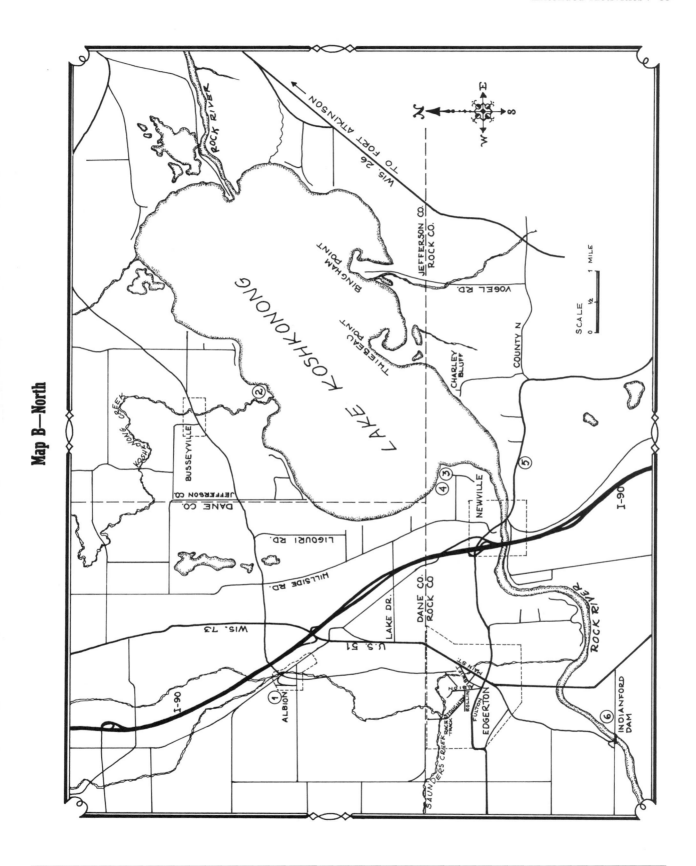

Map C—North

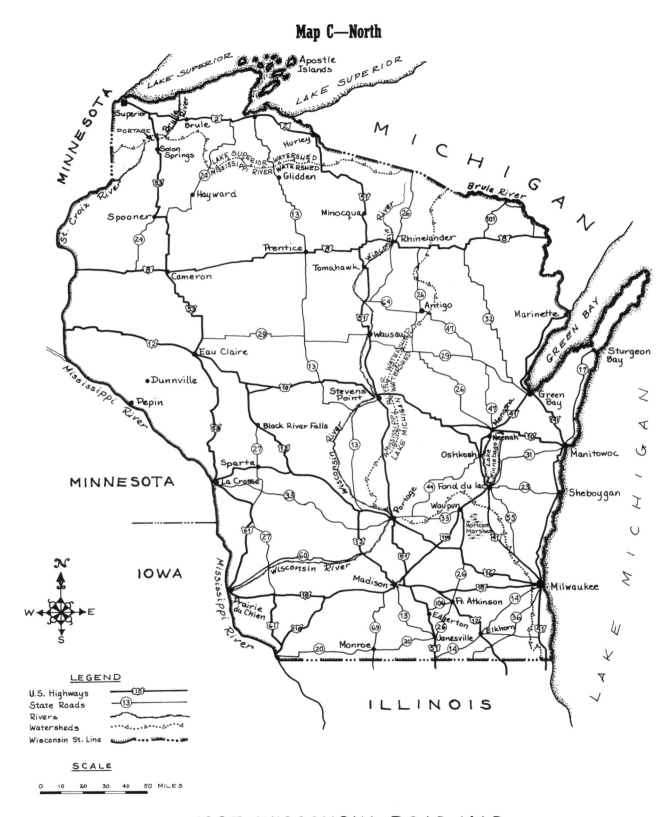

1927 WISCONSIN ROAD MAP

From *On Location*, 1992. Teacher Ideas Press, a Division of Libraries Unlimited, P.O. Box 6633, Englewood, CO 80155-6633

5. Sterling was surprised to discover that he and his father had crossed from one watershed to another in their journey to the north woods.

   a. On the 1927 map of Wisconsin (map C—North), find and mark the watershed line between those streams whose waters eventually empty into the Atlantic Ocean and those that flow into rivers that empty into the Gulf of Mexico.

   b. Suppose Sterling dropped a bottle containing a secret message into Saunders Creek. Using both Wisconsin and U.S. maps, plot the route of that bottle until it reaches the sea.

   c. Now suppose that on the trip to the North Woods he dropped a second bottle into Lake Winnebago. Trace the path of that bottle to the sea.

   d. When Sterling arrived at the Brule River, suppose he cast a third message adrift in a bottle. Follow its route to the sea.

   e. Would any of these messages eventually end up in the same body of water? Where would they meet?

6. Visit your public or school library and find a current road atlas. Use the atlas to plan a trip to Edgerton. Consider the following as you plan your trip:

   a. the most direct and fastest routes available between your town and Edgerton

   b. places of interest you might like to see along the way

   c. the estimated mileage for the round-trip journey

   d. total travel time and, if overnight stops will be necessary, possible places for those stays

   e. time zone changes along the way

7. Using a map that shows latitude and longitude, plot the location of Edgerton using those coordinates. Compare that location with the latitude and longitude of your hometown.

8. Using specialized maps, compare the climate, landforms, drainage, and vegetation in Edgerton and your hometown.

9. Compare the transportation, economy, and population density around Edgerton and in the region around your hometown.

10. When the students in Janesville discovered that the setting of one of their favorite books was in a nearby town, they took action to have Sterling North's home identified for others. Are there books that are set in your hometown? Are the settings identified so that readers can easily locate them?

11. The town of Edgerton is named for Benjamin Edgerton, the engineer in charge of building the railroad that came to town in 1853. At your school or public library, locate similar information on the history of your hometown. What is the origin of its name?

SUGGESTED READING

Other Books by Sterling North

Abe Lincoln: Log Cabin to White House. New York: Random House, 1956. 184 pages.
    Lincoln's boyhood and youth are carefully examined, and the events leading to his presidency are described.

George Washington, Frontier Colonel. New York: Random House, 1957. 184 pages.
    Washington's early life, especially his experiences in the French and Indian War, are detailed here.

Little Rascal. New York: Dutton, 1965. 78 pages.
    This is an abridged and especially illustrated version of *Rascal* that has been rewritten for young readers.

Mark Twain and the River. Boston: Houghton Mifflin, 1961. 184 pages.
    This accurate biography covers the well-known author's life from birth to death, and it is written in the mood of Twain's own books.

Raccoons Are the Brightest People. New York: Dutton Children's Books, 1966. 192 pages.
    This book deals with raccoon life around North's New Jersey farm.

So Dear to My Heart. New York: Doubleday, 1947. 240 pages.
    Here is the tale of an Indiana boy and his pet lamb. The story was later filmed by Walt Disney.

Thoreau of Walden Pond. Boston: Houghton Mifflin, 1958. 182 pages.
    This examination of Henry David Thoreau is set against the background of the New England countryside he loved.

The Wolfling. New York: Scholastic, 1980. 256 pages.
    This is the story of a Wisconsin boy in the 1870s, his growing love of nature, and of the wolf-dog he raises from a wild pup.

Young Thomas Edison. Boston: Houghton Mifflin, 1958. 182 pages.
    North describes how the life of this genius was amazingly productive, despite being fraught with turmoil and disappointment.

Wild Animal Pets (Fiction)

Byars, Betsy. *The Midnight Fox*. New York: Viking, 1968. 157 pages.
    Tommy is sent to spend a summer on a farm, where he is sure he will be miserable. He isn't athletic and he has a long list of fears. But when he sees a black fox, it is a beautiful, breathtaking experience. The wondrous thing is that he continues to see the fox, 15 times in all.

Eckert, Allan W. *Incident at Hawk's Hill*. Boston: Little, Brown, 1971. 173 pages.

Ben McDonald is six years old, but he is only the size of a three-year-old and is shy and peculiar as well. One day in 1870 he vanishes on the Canadian prairie around his home, and he is given up for dead. But Ben has the ability to observe carefully and to mimic wildlife. He is adopted by a female badger and lives in her den. Within a few months he has become wild, with only faint memories of his home and family.

George, Jean. *Cry of the Crow*. New York: Harper, 1980. 149 pages.

When a crow's nest is shot down, Nina finds a helpless baby crow. Her family considers crows pests that must be kept away from their strawberry farm, so Nina must secretly raise and train her new pet. She even learns to communicate with the bird.

_____. *My Side of the Mountain*. New York: Dutton, 1959. 178 pages.

Sam Gribley runs away from a crowded city apartment and spends a winter alone in the Catskill Mountains, with only his tamed peregrin falcon and other wildlife for company.

Morey, Walt. *Gentle Ben*. New York: Dutton, 1965. 191 pages.

Ben, an Alaskan brown bear, has been raised by a heartless man but then befriended and owned by young Mark Anderson. When Ben almost kills his former owner, Mark must fight to save his pet's life.

_____. *Sandy and the Rock Star*. New York: Dutton, 1979. 171 pages.

A 15-year-old runaway rock star and a giant cougar join forces to elude an eccentric millionaire who is obsessed with killing the cat.

Mowat, Farley. *Owls in the Family*. Boston: Little, Brown, 1961. 103 pages.

This is the true story of a Canadian boy who raises Wol and Weeps, two captive owls.

Rawlings, Marjorie Kinnan. *The Yearling*. New York: Macmillan, 1985. 403 pages.

Jody has raised Flag, a pet fawn, on his family's farm in the Florida scrub forest. When Flag grows up, Jody must make a tragic decision that forces him to mature, too.

Rogers, Jean. *The Secret Moose*. New York: Greenwillow, 1985. 64 pages.

Gerald secretly follows the trail of an injured moose and discovers her baby.

Wild Animal Pets (Nonfiction)

Kellner, Esther. *Animals Come to My House: A Story Guide to the Care of Small Wild Animals*. New York: Putnam, 1976. 160 pages.

The author describes five common woodland mammals she has cared for and provides instructions for taking care of orphaned baby animals. Shelter and diet are covered.

Weber, William. *Wild Orphan Babies: Mammals and Birds, Caring for Them, Setting Them Free*. New York: Holt, Rinehart and Winston. 1975. 159 pages.

A complete guide to caring for wild animals and birds that have been orphaned or abandoned by their natural parents and that are found by humans. Instructions on how to release the animals into their natural environment are also provided.

Canoeing

Barrett, Norman. *Canoeing*. New York: Watts, 1988. 32 pages.
Informative and colorful illustrations enhance this interesting book for young or reluctant readers.

Moran, Tom. *Canoeing Is for Me*. Minneapolis, MN: Lerner, 1984. 47 pages.
Two brothers take a canoe trip and demonstrate the skills needed on the journey.

Pensler, Otto. *Danger! White Water*. Troll, 1976. 32 pages.
This brief book for reluctant readers explores the thrills and excitement of canoeing on an angry river.

Chief Black Hawk

Anderson, La Vere. *Black Hawk*. Champaign, IL: Garrard, 1972. 80 pages.
A fictionalized biography that emphasizes Black Hawk's dedication to his people's heritage and his futile struggle to save their territory.

Gurko, Miriam. *Indian America: The Black Hawk War*. New York: Crowell, 1970. 223 pages.
Here is a detailed history of the tragic conflict between white men and suffering Indians who are forced from their land.

Oppenheim, Joanne. *Black Hawk: Frontier Warrior*. Troll, 1979. 48 pages.
This book explores the decision faced by Black Hawk: face hunger on a reservation or face enemy soldiers at home.

Wayne, Bennett. *Indian Patriots of the Eastern Woodlands*. Champaign, IL: Garrard, 1976. 167 pages.
Brief biographies of four Indian chiefs, including a section on Black Hawk and his people. There are several portraits of the chief and his people by George Catlin.

Fishing

Arnosky, Jim. *Flies in the Water, Fish in the Air: A Personal Introduction to Fly Fishing*. New York: Lothrop, Lee and Shepard, 1986. 96 pages.
Here is a well-illustrated how-to guide to the art of fly-fishing and to the natural world.

_____. *Freshwater Fish and Fishing*. New York: Macmillan, 1982. 63 pages.
A beginner's guide to fish and their habitat, plus practical advice on how to catch them.

Evanoff, Vlad. *A Complete Guide to Fishing*. New York: Crowell, 1981. 208 pages.
Tackle, bait, lures, types of fish, and sportsmanship are all covered in this book.

Roberts, Charles P. *Fishing for Fun: A Freshwater Guide*. Minneapolis, MN: Dillon, 1984. 155 pages.
Learn where and when to fish, how to clean fish, and many other things in this generously illustrated guide.

Thomas, Art. *Fishing Is for Me*. Minneapolis, MN: Lerner, 1980. 46 pages.
Fishing techniques, equipment, bait, and types of fish are explained by two young friends.

Loons

Billings, Charlene W. *The Loon*. New York: Dodd, Mead, 1988. 48 pages.
The loon's habits are explored. Outstanding photographs supplement the text.

Esbensen, Barbara Juster. *Great Northern Diver: The Loon*. Boston: Little, Brown, 1990. 32 pages.
The text is informative and the photographs are handsome in this portrayal of the loon.

Raccoons

Arnosky, Jim. *Raccoons and Ripe Corn*. New York: Lothrop, Lee and Shepard, 1987. unpaginated.
A mother raccoon and her two kits raid a cornfield one fall night and cause a good deal of destruction. An interesting view of the habits of raccoons, accompanied with beautiful illustrations.

Blassingame, Walter. *Wonders of Raccoons*. New York: Dodd, Mead, 1977. 80 pages.
Raccoons' interesting habits and physical characteristics are described by an author who has kept them as house pets. Illustrated with beautiful photographs.

MacClintock, Dorcas. *A Natural History of Raccoons*. New York: Scribner's, 1981.
A thorough study of the characteristics and habits of raccoons. Includes a chapter on caring for raccoons. Sterling North is frequently quoted, and Rascal's behavior is explained.

_____. *A Raccoon's First Year*. New York: Scribner's, 1982. 47 pages.
The development of a female baby raccoon from the time she is a week old to the day she gives birth to her own two cubs.

Nentl, Jerolyn Ann. *The Raccoon*. New York: Crestwood, 1984. 48 pages.
Color illustrations and interesting facts about habits and behavior are found in this brief study.

Patent, Dorothy Hinshaw. *Raccoons, Coatimundis, and Their Family*. New York: Holiday House, 1979. 127 pages.
The members of the family *Procyonidae* are introduced. Discussions of their environment, habits, and desirability as pets are included.

Rocks and Rock Collecting

Fichter, George S. *Rocks and Minerals*. New York: Random House, 1982.

Lampert, David. *Rocks and Minerals*. New York: Watts, 1986. 32 pages.
This short, colorfully illustrated book introduces rock types and specimen collecting.

McGowen, Tom. *Album of Rocks and Minerals*. New York: Macmillan, 1981. 61 pages.
Learn how to locate and identify various types of rocks. Information is also given on the properties and uses of many rocks and minerals.

Symes, R. F. *Rocks and Minerals*. New York: Knopf, 1988. 64 pages. Eyewitness Books series.
  Hundreds of color photographs illustrate a wide range of rocks and minerals, and information is provided on rock formation, erosion, and fossils.

Wisconsin History and Travel

Aylesworth, Thomas G. *Western Great Lakes: Illinois, Iowa, Minnesota, Wisconsin*. New York: Chelsea, 1987. 64 pages.
  A quick, well-illustrated reference work.

Bellville, Cheryl Walsh. *Farming Today Yesterday's Way*. Minneapolis, MN: Carolrhoda Books, 1984. 40 pages.
  In this book, much of the work on a small dairy farm in Wisconsin is done by draft horses rather than modern machines. A year on this unusual farm is depicted in photos and described in text that is easily read.

Gard, Robert E. *Wild Goose Marsh: Horicon Stopover*. Madison, WI: Stanton and Lee, 1975. 224 pages.
  This history of the marsh ranges from prehistory through pioneer times to the contemporary reclamation of this natural wonderland.

Stein, R. Conrad. *Wisconsin*. Chicago: Children's Press, 1987. 144 pages. America the Beautiful series.
  The geography, history, government, economy, arts and recreational features of the state are covered in this text, which contains full-color graphics.

World War I

Hoobler, Dorothy, and Thomas Hoobler. *An Album of World War I*. New York: Franklin Watts, 1976. 96 pages.
  A survey of the war, illustrated with numerous pictures. Maps show major battle lines and the territorial changes resulting from the war.

_____. *Trenches: Fighting on the Western Front in World War I*. New York: Putnam, 1978. 191 pages.
  Most of the fighting in World War I took place in the trenches. This book describes trench warfare, the new weapons developed, and the way of life of the soldiers in those trenches.

Marrin, Albert. *Yanks Are Coming: The United States in the First World War*. New York: Atheneum, 1986. 248 pages.
  The story of U.S. participation in World War I is told in black-and-white photos and detailed text.

Maynard, Christopher, and David Jefferis. *The Aces: Pilots and Planes of World War I*. New York: Watts, 1987. 31 pages.
  Some exciting air battles of World War I are described. Includes information on planes, insignia, and the top aces of eight countries.

Chapter 5 — Jasper County, Illinois:

The Setting for Irene Hunt's

Across Five Aprils

Follett, 1964. 190 pages.

BOOK SUMMARY

During the American Civil War, loyalties are divided in southern Illinois. Sometimes the conflict between the Union and the Confederacy extends down to the family level, sometimes with tragic consequences. Such is the case in the Creighton family. Originally hailing from Kentucky, they still have kin there, and they can readily understand the Southern point of view on states' rights. Yet they are against slavery and are strong supporters of their fellow Illinoisan, Abraham Lincoln.

In *Across Five Aprils* Jethro Creighton, the youngest in a large family, has just turned nine years old in 1861 and is only beginning to be aware of the problems of government and politics that loom over the country. The knotty issues of the day—issues Jethro tries hard to understand—are often discussed by his parents and older brothers.

When war comes to the fictional Creighton family, Jethro's 18-year-old brother Tom and cousin Eb Carron immediately join the Union army, both sure that the war will be short and bring them adventure and glory. John, the oldest of the Creighton boys, leaves his young wife and two little sons in his father's care when he also enlists to fight for the North.

Bill, Jethro's favorite brother, is a quiet, thoughtful young man who had puzzled his friends by joining the younger members of the family attending the one-room school recently built in the neighborhood. When Bill secretly leaves home, the family understands that he has followed his convictions to join "the Rebs." Now 14-year-old Jenny and Jethro are the only children that Matt and Ellen Creighton have left at home to help with work on the farm. An increasing burden of hard work falls on Jethro as he tries to take up the load of his absent brothers.

Each member of the family is caught up in the war. Shadrach Yale, Jethro's friend and school teacher, joins the Union forces and leaves behind an anxious and lonely Jenny, whom he had been courting. Matt had long opposed the romance between Jenny and Shad, feeling that Jenny was too young to consider marriage.

Shad's letters, along with those from the Creighton brothers, give a picture of the war that is far from the glory and drama that had been imagined by Eb and Tom. Here, as in the rest of the novel, the details of the war and the personalities involved are vividly described through eyewitness accounts sent in letters from the front to the family back home.

Passions grow strong in Jasper County, and a gang of local toughs single out the Creightons as Rebel sympathizers because of rumors that Bill is in the Confederate army. Jethro is harassed while on an errand in Newton and attacked as he returns home on a dark and lonely country road.

The war takes a tremendous financial, emotional, and physical toll on the Creightons in *Across Five Aprils*, and Matt Creighton falls ill, apparently the victim of a heart attack. Friends and neighbors fear that the Creightons have been labeled "Copperheads" and will become targets of violence. For a month volunteers stand watch at the cabin waiting for an attack, but it is not until after the protection ends that the destructive, secretive assault comes. First, the family dog disappears, then the farm well is fouled with coal oil in a midnight raid, and, on the same night, the barn is burned to the ground.

It is during the second April of the war that the Creightons learn that Tom had been killed at Pittsburg Landing in Tennessee. The news is brought to them by a neighbor boy, Dan Lawrence, who had been wounded and is returning from battle.

One night the family is visited by three men who claim to be representatives of the Federal Registrar who are charged with hunting down deserters from the United States Army. Army deserters had become a threat in the county; a large band of them had gathered at Point Prospect, a campground near Rose Hill, regularly terrorizing the neighborhood, stealing livestock and foodstuffs. The federal agents search the Creighton home and barn looking for Eb, whom they thought had deserted the Union ranks. The officials warned the family that they will be "up to [their] necks in trouble" if they harbor a deserter.

On a March day when working in a field some distance from the house, Jethro hears a cry like that of a wild turkey calling to him each time he passed a certain spot in the woods. When he investigates he finds Eb, starving and ragged. In order to protect the family, Jethro does not tell anyone of Eb's return and secretly supplies his cousin with food and blankets. Eb admits to making a mistake by leaving his post and he wishes he could somehow return to the army without being shot for desertion. After pondering the problem for some time, Jethro sends a letter to President Lincoln requesting a pardon for Eb. The response that arrives from Lincoln a few weeks later tells of an upcoming presidential order pardoning all deserters who return to their posts by April 1.

In July 1863 word arrives that Shadrach Yale has been seriously wounded at Gettysburg and is dying in a hospital in Washington. A family friend, Ross Milton, the editor of the Newton newspaper, offers to accompany Jenny to Washington if Matt will allow her to go. Matt agrees to the trip, and Jenny and Milton hastily begin the long journey. By August letters arrive from Jenny telling first of Shad's recovery and then of their marriage.

The war drags on dismally, and the end seems no nearer in 1864 than it did in 1861. In December a letter arrives from John telling of a chance meeting with Bill. John had been assigned the task of feeding Rebel prisoners taken in a recent clash at Nashville and he recognized his brother among the ragged, dirty captives. He was able to arrange some time alone with him, and the letter relates their conversation. It is the last the family hears of Bill.

Finally, in April 1865, the word comes that the war is over, but the news of Lincoln's assassination cuts the wild celebration painfully short. Jethro is in despair over the future of the country and for the loss of the man he considered his friend. Although he longs to go to the funeral in Springfield, he realizes that he could not spare the time away from the farm to travel the 100 miles to the state capitol. He is now the family's only provider and he accepts his responsibility with maturity.

A few days later Shad and Jenny arrive back at the farm, and Tom and Eb are expected to return shortly from the front. Shad and Jenny have made plans for the future, and those plans include Jethro. They invite Jethro to live with them and to continue his education. The last of the five Aprils brings the promise of happier times to come.

ABOUT THE AUTHOR

Irene Hunt was born near Newton, Illinois, in 1907. When she was a small child, her father contracted typhoid fever and died at the age of 36. For many years she lived on the farm that had been in her family for generations.

Miss Hunt began teaching English and French in the Oak Park, Illinois, public schools in 1930 while pursuing her bachelor's degree at the University of Illinois, from which she graduated in 1939. In 1945 she left Oak Park and attended the University of Minnesota, receiving her master's degree in 1946. For the next four years she was an instructor of psychology at the University of South Dakota. In 1950 Irene Hunt returned to Illinois and taught junior high in Cicero until 1965, when she became the district director of language arts. During her tenure, she was noted for her ability to instill in students and teachers her own enthusiasm for great books and the happiness and enlightenment that they bring.

Miss Hunt had been pounding the typewriter and collecting rejection slips for many years when, to critical acclaim, her first novel was published in 1964. She was 57 years old. That novel was *Across Five Aprils* and it was immediately hailed as intriguing and beautifully written. Recipient of the Charles Follett Award (1964), the Dorothy Canfield Fisher and the Clara Ingram Judson Memorial Awards (1965), and the Lewis Carroll Shelf Award (1966), *Across Five Aprils* was the only Newbery Honor book in 1965.

Her next book, *Up a Road Slowly*, published in 1966, seems so real that it is often identified as semiautobiographical. In this story of a young girl's growth to maturity, however, only the first chapter and one other episode are based on personal reminiscence. The novel won the Newbery Medal for 1967.

Miss Hunt continued to write books for young people, even after her retirement near Clearwater, Florida. Her last book was *The Everlasting Hills* published in 1985. Miss Hunt plans to return to Illinois and live in Champaign, less than 100 miles north of Jasper County.

SETTING: JASPER COUNTY, ILLINOIS

The Creightons and the Lands

In the "Author's Note" at the end of *Across Five Aprils*, Irene Hunt says that the story was suggested by the tales she heard from her grandfather, James Land, and from family records and letters. Many years later she admitted that, since so many young people took her remarks literally, she wished she had not implied that those events actually happened. Although the names of places are all very accurately reported in the book, the characters are all fictitious. The parallels between the fictional Creighton family and the real Lands are, however, very interesting to explore.

The story is developed using Miss Hunt's family home east of Hidalgo, in Jasper County, Illinois. Her grandfather, James Land, was, like Jethro Creighton, just nine years old in 1861. Like Jethro he was part of a large family; there were nine children listed in the Jasper County census of 1860, and the oldest boy had already grown and moved away. Like the Creightons, the Lands came from Kentucky.

According to those census records the father, William H. Land, was born in Kentucky in 1809, and his wife in 1814 in the same state. Other county records show that one son, John, was born to the couple in Kentucky in 1832. Four years later the little family moved to Decatur County, Indiana, where five more children were born; William in 1839, Mary in 1842, Sarah in 1844, Thomas in 1845, and Morgan in 1850.

In 1850 William Land purchased 80 acres of prairie in the Crooked Creek Township of Jasper County, Illinois, on the western edge of the woods that rimmed that creek. James Land was born in 1852, and the next year his oldest brother, John, married Nancy Ellis. John and Nancy lived on the family farm until 1855.

Clearly, Irene Hunt borrowed from the Lands the names and the family position for her characters in *Across Five Aprils*. The brothers John, Bill, and Tom all appear in the book and in that age order, and Nancy is the name of the fictional John Creighton's wife. In the book, Mary Creighton, the beautiful older sister, was killed in an accident in 1859.

Miss Hunt also closely adhered to actual locations in the area of the Land homestead. The nearest settlement, less than a mile down the road, was the community of Point Pleasant. There was a church, a general store, and a one-room schoolhouse. The Land children, like the Creightons, walked to that schoolhouse; the 1860 census shows that while mother Jane Land, like Ellen Creighton, could neither read nor write, five of her children had attended school the previous year.

James Land married Mary Ault in 1880, and they began their life together on the old Land farm. Their daughter Sarah was Irene Hunt's mother. Sarah Land married the Point Pleasant schoolmaster Franklin Hunt, and a family member speculates that the Jenny of the novel was based upon Sarah, James Land's daughter. James did object to the marriage of Sarah and Franklin, claiming that Sarah was too young, just as Matt Creighton objects to the romance of Jenny and Shad in the novel. The character of Shadrach Yale is drawn with such tenderness and admiration that it is suspected that Miss Hunt was actually describing her own schoolmaster father, who died when she was still a child.

Irene Hunt said that by the time she knew her grandfather, James Land, he had spent most of his time reliving the war years, and since he was a very good storyteller, he gave his listening grandchildren a wealth of detail that made it possible for them to share in the anxiety and sorrow of the times, as well as the happiness that touched the closely knit family. His storytelling ability is evident not only in the memory of his granddaughter but in other records as well. A diary he kept from 1905 through 1907 has been preserved by his heirs. In it he names events, friends, and neighbors and describes the activities that filled his busy days. The entries reveal a devoted family man who was interested in community affairs, a helpful friend and neighbor, and an industrious businessman involved in all aspects of farming and in a variety of local commercial ventures.

An interesting story is related about James Land. At one time he was in the Missouri Ozarks traveling by wagon when he was accosted along the road by a band of local roughnecks. He picked up a short piece of metal pipe from the floor of his wagon, stepped down, and prepared to defend himself. The leader of the toughs was impressed by his courage and complimented him on his bravery. James was allowed to continue on his way, unharmed. It is intriguing to speculate about whether this incident was reflected in the attack on Jethro imagined by James's granddaughter in her book many years later.

Irene Hunt has said that she long ago lost count of the number of times she had been asked if Bill ever returned home and she had to respond that there was no Bill of the Confederate forces, but only a name in her family tree.

In the midst of the prairie, just a few miles from the family farm, is the Swick Cemetery where members of the Land family are buried, including James and his parents, William and Jane (see fig. 5.1). Names can be found on other gravestones, some of which are the same as the names of characters in the novel *Across Five Aprils*.

FIG. 5.1. Swick Cemetery.

Jasper County in the 1860s

The presidential election of Abraham Lincoln of Illinois had brought the turmoil into the open; slavery and secession often formed the basis for arguments in homes, stores, and the press. Southern Illinois had been heavily settled by families from Kentucky, as well as many families from Ohio, causing sentiment to be divided between support of the North and the South.

Hunt paints a picture of a rural area torn asunder by the war, with mistrust and suspicion dividing the county. The *New and Complete History of Jasper County and the 1884 History of Jasper County* published in 1974 by Unigraphic, Inc., and edited by Glenn W. Sutherland, supports her description. According to that document most of the county residents were staunch Unionists who worked hard to support the soldiers in the field and the sick and wounded in the hospitals.[1] The ladies aid and sewing societies provided homemade supplies and gifts to the soldiers.

On the other hand, some of those Jasper County settlers who had originally come from the South were strong in their loyalties too. Emotions ranged from secret rebellion to outright murder. The southern sympathizers banded together in a unit of "The Knights of the Golden Circle," a semimilitary group with chapters throughout the Midwest. The organization soon became known as the Copperheads, and their purpose was to oppose the war efforts of the North through discouraging enlistments in the Union army and encouraging draft evasion and desertion. The story of the deserters' camp at Point Prospect is, apparently, based on fact, although it is not mentioned in the 1884 county history. According to local historians there was an area of deep woods with a creek nearby that harbored disreputable characters most of the time and, during the Civil War years, it became a refuge for men escaping from the conflict.

Army desertion was a widespread problem by 1863. Local legend places a Civil War deserters' camp at the wooded area southwest of Rose Hill near the Embarras River, as pictured in figure 5.2. Even today the area has the reputation of being a rough place, suspected as a hangout for unsavory characters.

FIG. 5.2. Location of the Civil War deserters' camp.

Fear and anger were rampant in the county, but the vicious acts of terror that followed were not committed by the Copperheads, but by local hoodlums and roving bands of ne'er-do-wells who saw in the unsettled situation a chance to vent their hate on the community. They attacked and beat those who unsuspectingly traveled on lonely, wooded roads. They viciously terrorized women whose husbands were in the battlefield, often killing their livestock and then trying to make it appear as if their ruthless deeds were committed by Copperheads.

The flat landscape of Jasper County, pictured in figure 5.3, is laced with streams that have sloping, forested banks. The Embarras River, with its once heavily wooded edges, dominates the area. The river was named by the French who settled in Vincennes, Indiana, and who referred to the river in French as "embarras," meaning "obstruction." Later pioneers referred to it as the "Ambraw," and so it is called today.

FIG. 5.3. This map shows the probable route Jethro took to town. The details given in the book for his encounters along the way do not accurately fit the actual distances. How has the author fictionalized reality to enhance the plot?

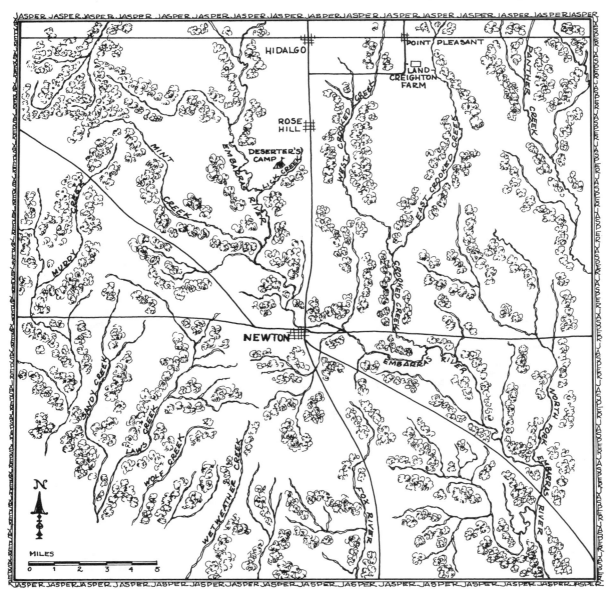

The settlers in the county chose to build their homes along the edges of the woodland, farming the prairie and using the timber for their log cabins and fuel. The forests and prairies held an abundance of wild game, and the streams were full of fish.

John Land followed the pioneer pattern when he came to Jasper County in 1850. The 80 acres he chose was close to the deep woods that mark the path of Crooked Creek, but opened to the prairie on the west (see fig. 5.4). A modern farmhouse is now located where the log cabin once stood, but a sign erected in 1972 (fig. 5.5) alerts passersby that

This Is a Centennial Farm
Owned by Same Family Over 100 Years

The farm is no longer owned by members of the Land family or by any of their descendants.

FIG. 5.4. The site of the Land farm.

FIG. 5.5. Marker stating that the farm had belonged to the Lands for 100 years.